Grief a

ONE WEEK LOAN

Grief and its Challenges

Neil Thompson

palgrave
macmillan

First published 2012 by
PALGRAVE MACMILLAN

Palgrave Macmillan in the UK is an imprint of Macmillan Publishers Limited,
registered in England, company number 785998, of Houndmills, Basingstoke,
Hampshire RG21 6XS.

Palgrave Macmillan in the US is a division of St Martin's Press LLC,
175 Fifth Avenue, New York, NY 10010.

Palgrave Macmillan is the global academic imprint of the above companies
and has companies and representatives throughout the world.

Palgrave® and Macmillan® are registered trademarks in the United States,
the United Kingdom, Europe and other countries.

ISBN 978–0–230–27756–4

This book is printed on paper suitable for recycling and made from fully
managed and sustained forest sources. Logging, pulping and manufacturing
processes are expected to conform to the environmental regulations of the
country of origin.

A catalogue record for this book is available from the British Library.

A catalog record for this book is available from the Library of Congress.

10   9   8   7   6   5   4   3   2   1
21   20   19   18   17   16   15   14   13   12

Printed in China

For Ron and Donna

Contents

List of Figures

Preface

The overall aim of the book is to provide a clearly written, well-informed introduction to the complex and demanding subject of grief to serve as a foundation for further study and professional practice.

In writing the book I had a number of objectives in mind, specifically:

(i)   To provide a basic introduction to grief as an inevitable feature of human experience;

(ii) To demonstrate that grief is a much more common experience than most people realize by showing that grief arises from a wide range of loss experiences and not just from bereavement;

(iii) To provide a critique of oversimplified theories of grief that rely on a reductionist stages model or medicalized understandings of human responses to loss;

(iv) To present a more sophisticated theoretical understanding of grief that does justice to the complexities involved;

(v)   To show how grief often underpins a range of psychological and social problems;

(vi) To show how grief can be 'transformational' – that is, a positive (albeit painful) source of growth and development; and

(vii) To provide guidance on how best to support people who are wrestling with the challenges of grief.

You would, of course, be right to assume that this is an awful lot to squeeze into one relatively short book. But my plan has been to provide a broad sketch of the landscape of grief in order to counterbalance the all-too-frequent tendency to focus too narrowly on grief – in particular, to adopt a (bio-)psychological view that neglects sociological aspects and which often has little to say about spiritual dimensions.

By adopting this broad focus I am hoping to show how extensive an issue grief is and will, in the process, also emphasize how complex it is. A key 'message' of the book, then, is to warn against the dangers of narrow and oversimplified approaches. From a theoretical point of view, these can prevent us from developing an understanding of grief that does justice to the complexities involved. From a practice perspective, they can lead to a distorted picture of the situations we are dealing with which, in turn, can result in not only a failure to be helpful, but also, in some circumstances, making the problems and suffering worse.

Who is the book for?

This book will appeal primarily to students and professional practitioners across the helping professions (social work and social care; medicine and health care; youth and community work; child welfare; counselling and psychotherapy; ministry and pastoral guidance), especially – but not exclusively – those whose work brings them into regular contact with dying or bereaved people. There will also be much of interest to other professional groups, such as police and other emergency services personnel, as well as teachers and other child care workers (play workers, foster carers and so on). Furthermore, there are many people outside the professional arena who could find the book of value – for example, hospice volunteers. I am also aware that many grieving people use the literature around grief as a form of 'bibliotherapy', and so they too may find that the book has considerable appeal for them. The same can also apply to people who are supporting someone who is grieving – friends, relatives and colleagues who may feel helpless in the face of such intense emotion and such significant difficulties.

What is distinctive about the book?

There are various ways in which this book differs from other texts available. In particular, it offers the following:

- A *critical* perspective on grief theory – much of the literature (and associated practice) relies on an uncritical acceptance of outdated and discredited theoretical perspectives that can distort our understanding of the situations we encounter;
- A *broad* perspective on grief, not limited to death-related losses;
- A *holistic* perspective on grief – that is, one that is psychosocial (it combines psychological and sociological insights) and spiritual in its scope, rather than narrow and individualistic in its focus; much of the current literature lacks a sociological dimension and some of it also lacks a spiritual dimension;
- An *exploration* of how grief – especially 'complicated' or trauma-related grief – often underpins psychological and social problems;
- An *examination* of 'transformational' grief as a basis for personal growth and empowerment – recognizing that, while grief brings many demands and potential problems, it also brings the potential for personal development and better ways of coping with life's challenges;
- A *blend* of theory and practice – many of the texts available fall into either the highly theoretical or technical category or the practical 'how to' category, but relatively few do a good job of *integrating* theory and practice;
- A *balance* of intellectual credibility and emotional sensitivity – parallel with the blend of theory and practice (much of the material available is rational and theoretical and has little to say about the emotional sensitivities involved, while other texts show great emotional sensitivity but make little or no reference to the theory base).

How do I use the book?

This is a relatively short book, but one which covers a lot of ground. To make the most of what it has to offer I would recommend that you read it through once to get the overview of the subject matter it addresses. You can then go back and re-read the chapters that appeal to you most – and, of course, different readers will have different interests. As you read through, whether first time or second, you are likely to find it helpful to be thinking about how what you are learning can be of help to you – about how the ideas can inform your practice; how they can help you prepare for an assignment and/or make sense of your own experiences of loss and grief.

Each chapter ends with some 'points to ponder'. I am aware that some readers find these helpful to pull their thoughts together and to review what they have just read, while others get little or no benefit from them. Different people learn in different ways, so you are free to make use of these questions or not, as you see fit. Similarly, each chapter has 'practice focus' illustrations and 'voice of experience' examples. These are not intended as in-depth case studies (although some tutors or trainers may benefit from using them as the basis of classroom exercises if they wish). Rather, they are intended as cameos that help to bring the issues to life, short examples that provide additional food for thought and help to provide links between theory and practice. Again, I am aware that some people find these very helpful – they suit their particular style of learning – while others tend to just skip over them and read on. So, it is quite simple really: if you find them useful, use them; if you do not, then there is no problem in passing them by. However, it is important not to simply assume in advance that you will not find them helpful. Give them a try and then decide on an informed basis.

Last but not least in terms of making best use of the book: one important thing to bear in mind is that no one reading this book will have been untouched by its subject matter. Loss and grief are part and parcel of being human, so it is not possible to remain completely dispassionate about what you are about to read, futile to try and be one hundred per cent objective about what it covers. At times, then, the book may remind you of one or more painful experiences of grief that have featured in your life. If this happens, then please do not assume that there is anything wrong with this, that you are, in some way, failing to 'do it properly'. Grief is, in some ways an echo of love, in the sense that, if we had not loved in the first place, there would be no sense of loss when we part company with the person or thing we have lost. So, when we are reminded of loss, we should also remember the love. As a friend of mine commented after his mother passed away: 'The reason I feel so bad is that she made me feel so good.'

Acknowledgements

I want to divide the people I owe gratitude to into three groups. In terms of the first group of people, those I am grateful to for helping to form the learning on which I have based this book, if I were to provide a comprehensive list it would take up several pages. I must therefore limit myself to a general acknowledgement to those people I have learned from through discussion, reading their work and listening to their contributions to conferences and workshops. This includes, but is not limited to, members of the International Work Group on Death, Dying and Bereavement, of which I have had the good fortune to have been a member for some 15 years.

The second category of people to whom I owe a debt of thanks are those who have been more personally involved in the development of my understanding and who have supported me in various ways. These are Donna O'Toole and Ron Abraham (to whom this book is dedicated in recognition of their friendship and the immense learning I have gained from spending a lot of time with them); Sid and Miriam Moss (to whom my *Loss, Grief and Trauma in the Workplace* book was dedicated); Gerry Cox and Bob Bendiksen, both formerly of the University of Wisconsin-La Crosse; Dick Gilbert of Mercy College, New York and the World Pastoral Care Center; and my very good friends, Denise Bevan of St Rocco's Hospice, Warrington, Jan Pascal of La Trobe University, Australia and Bernard Moss, Emeritus Professor at Staffordshire University.

The third category of people that I am indebted to are those who have played a key role in bringing this book to fruition. Of course, top of that list must be Susan Thompson who once again has been a tower of strength in various ways. Maggie Holloway once again did an excellent job as an audio-typist – a real beacon of quality work and reliability in a world where these features are often absent. Penny Simmons has also come to feature as a regular tower of strength as part of my support system due to the very high quality of her copyediting work, her excellent understanding of the writer's perspective and the friendly and helpful way she goes about her work. Dr Sharon Brimfield-Edwards was kind enough to read an earlier draft of the book and was able to provide some helpful comments. Catherine Gray at the publishers has continued to be an excellent colleague and source of support for this and other projects I have been involved with. Her backing for this particular book has been even stronger than her usually very high level of encouragement, and so I hope that it lives up to expectation for her, for everyone else who has played a part and for those who come to read the book in search of help in dealing with one of the most demanding aspects of being human.

About the author

Dr Neil Thompson is an independent author, trainer and consultant, working with Avenue Consulting Ltd (www.avenueconsulting. co.uk). He has held full or honorary professorships at four UK universities and has established himself as one of the leading thinkers and writers in his field. He has over 150 publications to his name, including best-selling textbooks, papers in learned journals and training and open learning materials. His recent books include:

> *Promoting Workplace Learning* (Policy Press, 2006)
> *Power and Empowerment* (Russell House Publishing, 2007)
> *The Critically Reflective Practitioner* (with Sue Thompson, Palgrave Macmillan, 2008)
> *Loss, Grief and Trauma in the Workplace* (Baywood, 2009)
> *People Skills* (3rd edn, Palgrave Macmillan, 2009)
> *Effective Communication* (2nd edn, Palgrave Macmillan, 2011)
> *Crisis Intervention* (2nd edn, Russell House, 2011)
> *Promoting Equality* (3rd edn, Palgrave Macmillan, 2011).

He has also produced a number of education and training DVDs (including one on *Working with Grief*), self-help audio programmes, training manuals and e-books (see www.avenuemediasolutions.com for more details). He has also set up a companion website for this book at www.griefchallenges.com <http://www.griefchallenges.com>.

Neil has over 34 years' experience as a practitioner, manager, educator, consultant and expert witness in the human services. He is very well respected for his ability to communicate complex ideas in an accessible way without oversimplifying them.

He has been a speaker at seminars and conferences in the UK, Ireland, Greece, the Netherlands, Norway, Italy, Spain, the Czech Republic, Hong Kong, India, Canada, the United States and Australia, and has qualifications in social work, management

(MBA), training and development, mediation and dispute resolution, as well as a first-class honours degree in Social Sciences, a doctorate (PhD) and a higher doctorate (DLitt).

Neil is a Fellow of the Chartered Institute of Personnel and Development; the Royal Society of Arts (elected on the basis of his contribution to workplace learning); and the Higher Education Academy; and a Life Fellow of the Institute of Welsh Affairs. In addition, he is a member of the International Work Group on Death, Dying and Bereavement.

He has served as the editor of the US-based international journal *Illness, Crisis & Loss*, and currently also edits the free *Well-being* **BULLETIN** e-zine (www.well-being.org.uk). He also founded the self-help website, *humansolutions* (www.humansolutions.org.uk).

He is now a sought-after workshop facilitator, consultant and conference speaker. His website (with a blog and a free 'tip of the week' facility) is at www.neilthompson.info.

Introduction

What is this book about?

Grief is an experience that none of us can escape. Many people try to gloss over their grief and allow it to touch them as little as possible, which is perfectly understandable, given how intensely painful grief can be. For many other people this is not possible. The extent, intensity and/or complexity of their grief are so overwhelming that they feel the need to abandon themselves to it. There is no right answer as to what the 'correct' way to grieve is, as it is a different path for everybody, albeit – as we shall see – with certain common elements. Grief is an existential challenge, by which I mean that it is a part of life (part of what it means to exist as a human being, hence the term, 'existential') that we all have to face up to, sooner or later. While it would be both unhelpful and unwise to try to give instructions or prescriptions about how to grieve (or how to help others cope with their grief), there are none the less important lessons that we can learn about the nature of grief, the challenges it brings and the various ways we can attempt to respond to those challenges. This book is about exploring those lessons, a point to which I shall return below.

This, then, is not a book that tells you how to grieve or helps you to tell others how to do it – the reality of grief is far too complex for that, and a tendency to oversimplify such matters runs the very real risk of making the pain and suffering of the experience all the more acute. It also prevents us from appreciating what is involved in loss experiences and holds us back from developing the sort of sophisticated level of understanding we need in order to do justice to the complexities and subtleties involved. This book is about helping to develop a sufficiently sophisticated understanding of what happens when we encounter one or more major losses in our life and are confronted with extremely powerful emotions.

But it is not just a matter of understanding grief 'from the inside', as it were, from the perspective of our own grief experiences. It is also important to look at how members of the helping professions, broadly defined, need to understand how to help and support people who are grieving (especially people who are struggling to cope with their losses in ways that go above and beyond the demands of 'ordinary grief' – what we shall refer to in Chapter 7 as experiences of 'complicated grief'). Understanding how we ourselves experience grief is a good starting point for being a supportive and empathic professional, but it is not enough on its own. This is because different people grieve in different ways – as I mentioned above, we all follow our own path. This book is about how we can help people to meet the challenges of grief, when they need such help.

The qualifying phrase 'when they need such help' is an important one. This is because we should not assume that grief is a 'problem' in need of a 'solution' or an 'illness' in need of a 'cure'. In the majority of cases there is no need for professional help – people manage to get by perfectly well without the need to call upon the services of one or other helping professional. See Furedi (2004) for an interesting and important discussion of the dangers of overgeneralizing the need for professional help. This book is about learning how to know when people need professional help and when they simply need the support of the people who care about them.

No single book – especially a short, introductory one like this – can provide all you need to know about grief. It therefore needs to be recognized that this book is not comprehensive or all-encompassing. However, what it should do is give you a clear understanding of how complex grief is; how much more common it is than people generally realize (especially the grief that arises from non-death-related losses); how devastating it can be if people are not given the help they need when they need it; and how much of a positive contribution a committed, sensitive, knowledgeable and skilful professional can make. It should also give you a desire to find out more, to build on your existing knowledge and understanding. This book is therefore about stimulating an interest in taking the introductory understanding offered here to more advanced levels through further reading, discussion and practice.

The challenges of grief

The challenges presented by grief can be seen to operate at two levels. First, there are the challenges involved in any significant loss and subsequent grief reaction:

- The emotional 'storm' that we are likely to face – any (shifting) combination of anger, sadness, bitterness, fear, regret, disappointment, hopelessness, depression, panic and confusion.
- Managing to 'go on' – trying to live our lives while facing such a storm: holding down a job, bringing up our children, supporting others in our circle who are grieving the same loss, and so on.
- Keeping safe – the confusion, disorientation and distress of a major loss can lead to major difficulties in terms of concentration and focus. We can therefore present a risk to ourselves and others in terms of driving, operating machinery at work, using electrical devices at home and so on. The significance of the risks involved should not be underestimated.
- Rebuilding our lives – practically, emotionally and spiritually; making the (often major) adjustments we need to come to terms with the changes to our life that the loss has brought about.
- Where the loss has been the loss of someone we love, learning to love again, learning to trust others with our feelings, rather than protecting ourselves from future grief by refusing to enter into a loving relationship.
- Similarly, where the loss has involved the loss of trust or security, learning to trust people and feel safe again, not allowing the hurt of the loss to cut us off from other people and the benefits of 'connectedness' (see below for a discussion of this).

Second, there are the *additional* challenges we face when grief is problematic or 'complicated' in some way (for example, when there is also an element of psychological trauma involved). These include, but are not limited to, avoiding:

- A vicious circle of stress and distress that can have a major impact on mental health and well-being, possibly leading to the stigma of a psychiatric label being applied;
- A vicious circle of events: losing our job; encountering financial difficulties as a result of this; losing our home and perhaps also family as a consequence of the intense strains on family life; and so on.
- Alienating the people who can be supportive and helpful (for example, if someone's grieving manifests itself as aggression or hostility towards people).
- Engaging in destructive or self-destructive behaviour as a counterproductive way of dealing with the pressures we are facing.
- Losing all hope and settling for a life of unhappiness and despair.

In addition, there is the further challenge of trying to make our grief experience a 'transformational' one, trying to make the most of the silver lining by using the loss, however painful and distressing, to help us grow and develop and be better prepared for any future losses or life challenges we will encounter (Calhoun and Tedeschi, 2001). This is an important topic to which we will return in Chapter 1.

These are just some of the main challenges loss and grief present for all of us, but there are also the challenges of being a helper in supporting other people in dealing with their grief. These challenges include:

- *Maintaining a balance of sensitivity.* That is, being sensitive and understanding (empathic), without allowing our own feelings of pain and hurts associated with our own losses to take over. This is a challenge of emotional intelligence – being able to 'read' people's emotions so that we understand as best we can, being 'in touch' with our own feelings, but keeping a balance, so that we are neither insensitive nor emotionally overinvolved. This can be a very difficult challenge at times, but it is none the less a vitally important one. Because it is so important, then, there is no problem about seeking support in relation to such matters as and when you need it. Emotional intelligence is not about being 'macho' or pretending we do not have feelings. It is about learning how to keep them in perspective, and the guidance of a supportive colleague or manager can be very helpful in this regard.

- *Dealing with our own feelings of helplessness.* One of the most important lessons we can learn about helping people who are grieving is that we cannot take their pain away. This can mean at times that we feel quite helpless, wishing there was something that we could do to make the pain cease. It is important, then, to note that there are things we can do to help, and that this can help to ease the suffering involved, even if it cannot actually stop the process from being painful.

- *Maintaining a balance of involvement.* Grieving people can appear helpless at times, and so we must resist the temptation to take over. The presence of grief in a situation does not suspend the importance of the need to work in partnership where possible. As indicated above, we also need to be clear about which grief-related situations require professional help and which do not.

- *Avoiding exhaustion.* Grief tends to be a very tiring experience, emotionally, physically and spiritually draining. This can rub off on professional helpers who, if they do not take the lessons of self-care seriously, can find themselves exhausted and possibly on the way to burnout.

This is by no means an exhaustive list, but it should be enough to paint a picture of the challenging nature of being a professional helper supporting people through grief, especially if you are a worker who specializes in this type of work.

However, challenges also bring rewards. Professional helpers can play a hugely helpful role in making a positive difference to people when they are at their most vulnerable. For example, we can help to create a sense of sanctuary when people are feeling very unsafe and insecure. Smith and Smith (2008) give us some helpful insights into what is involved:

> Helpers ... have a particular role to play in creating environments in which powerful feelings of fear and pain can be contained. They may well try to create places of sanctuary, spaces where people can feel safe. One aspect of this is people having some sense that they are away from the things that cause them pain or concern. Here they need the other people in the setting to treat them with respect, to be tolerant, and to give them room. An important feature of this for helpers is to acknowledge people's pain and difficulties, but not to push and prod unnecessarily. Sanctuary doesn't involve sweeping issues under the carpet, but rather creating the conditions so that people can talk when they are ready. This often involves helpers in treading a fine line between quietness and encouraging conversation. Often powerful feelings are contained because people feel they are with someone who is safe, who will not condemn them for the emotions they are experiencing or the things they have done. (pp. 84–5)

There are, of course, no magic answers to helping people through grief, but it would be unduly pessimistic and defeatist to assume that there is little or nothing we can do. A sensitive, skilled, knowledgeable and committed professional helper can sometimes be the difference between someone coping and not being able to cope, or between just about coping and getting the full benefits of transformational grief.

One of the important considerations that can help us move in the right direction is the recognition that grieving can best be understood as a process of healing, and so it is worth exploring what this involves.

Grief as healing

Significant losses in our lives cause deep and intense pain. It can even go so far as to 'wound' us, which is when we would use the term 'trauma' and talk or write about 'traumatic grief' ('trauma' being the Greek word for wound). We will explore these issues in more depth in Chapter 2, but for now it is important to note that any form of grief can be seen as a process of healing, of 'mending' the hurt.

It is important not to assume that, because we are using a term that is often associated with health and medicine that we are viewing grief as an illness. A grieving person is not a 'sick' person in any literal sense. However, there will be psychological, social and spiritual aspects of loss that we will need to address, and it is in this broader metaphorical sense that we are using the term 'healing'. It is a case of 'healing':

- *The emotional hurt.* The emotional pain can be both extensive and intensive, leaving us feeling emotionally devastated. It can take a long time to get our feelings and moods back into balance. What makes this particularly complex is that the range of feelings involved is very wide and the emotional landscape can keep changing, in the sense that, at times, some emotions will feature more than others.
- *The social damage.* As I shall emphasize later in the book, there is a significant social dimension to loss and grief that is often neglected in the grief literature and accepted wisdom. It is therefore important to note that there can be significant social costs that can feature in our lives when we encounter one or more major losses.
- *The spiritual hurt.* Our sense of who we are and how we fit into the wider world; our sense of personal safety and security; and our feeling of 'connection' to other people and the wider world can all be significantly undermined by a loss. It can take a lot of time – and sometimes help – to heal the hurt involved. Many people find their religious faith to be a great help to them at such times.

One of the important implications of understanding grief as a process of healing is that we need to learn not to see grief as a problem in itself. The idea that something is a problem suggests that we should start looking for solutions, and there are, of course, no solutions to grief, only the painful, exhausting, frightening and confusing journey of healing. In most situations people need only the people who care about them to accompany them on that journey. However, at times, people need more than that – whether it is because they have no one to care for them due to their social isolation, or the nature of their loss(es) is such that professional help is needed (for example, traumatic losses or grief experiences that are otherwise 'complicated' in some way).

Responding to the challenges

Helping people to 'heal' is basically the key to helping people respond to the challenges involved in grief. However, that simple statement masks a set of very complex issues, as helping someone 'heal' is not necessarily a simple or straightforward process. It requires a substantial knowledge base, considerable skills, great sensitivity and a degree of commitment. This book will not provide you with all these, but it should play an important part in taking you in the right direction.

So, in this book you will not find simple solutions or sets of prescriptions for practice. What you will find, though, is an account of many of the demanding, but fascinating, aspects of the world we enter when we attempt to help people deal with their grief challenges. That account should give you some insights and, ideally, motivate you to find out more, to keep on learning.

It should also alert you to the significant challenges involved for the professional helper, not to discourage and dishearten you, but to prepare you for what you need to do (and what you need to learn) to be the best professional helper you can be in addressing some issues that are very demanding, but also very rewarding – for the people you are helping, but also for yourself in terms of job satisfaction and professional enrichment. De Unamuno made the point many years ago that 'Although this meditation upon mortality may soon induce in us a sense of anguish, it fortifies us in the end' (1954, p. 42 – originally published 1921). We can extend this wisdom beyond mortality to encompass loss and grief more broadly.

In facing these challenges we need to recognize that we are not alone. Part of what we can do to help grieving people is to help them realize that they are not alone, that there are people who are 'there for them'. The same logic applies. We have to be aware that facing the significant challenges of supporting people through grief should not be a solitary undertaking. We should seek out – and use – the support of those people we know we can rely on to guide and protect us through potentially difficult times. If we feel we do not have such people to rely on, then that is a key lesson in itself: the need to take whatever steps are necessary to secure the support we need, rather than run the risk of entering difficult and demanding territory without appropriate back up when we need it.

At the very least, we may need support to deal with the anxieties and fears involved with dealing with grief and loss. As Smith and Smith (2008) comment:

> If we aspire to connect with humanity and have this as the basis of our practice, we need to put aside our fear of engaging with the rawness of life and instead embrace it. This is something that Palmer highlights. He argues that if we reclaim the connectedness of life we take away the fear of connecting (1998, p58). (p. 39)

Connectedness is an important concept that I will draw on from time to time. It has emerged from our understanding of spirituality and our appreciation that spirituality involves a sense of being connected to other people, of being part of something bigger than ourselves – in a sense, a feeling of being part of humankind, rather than just an isolated individual in our own private world. Experiences of loss and grief can make us want to withdraw into our own private world, but this can often mean that we lose out on the benefits of 'connectedness', of being part of a shared human family.

One further important point to take on board in considering rising to the challenges involved is the role of critically reflective practice. I made the point earlier that we need to learn the lessons of the nature of loss, the challenges involved and the potential ways of helping. I stand by that point, but want to emphasize that it needs to be understood as part of critically reflective practice (S. Thompson and N. Thompson, 2008). What I mean by this is that it is not simply a matter of reading about what steps you need to take, as if it were just a process of following a particular procedure or protocol. Working with loss involves dealing with people, and that means, of course, that there will be complications, contradictions and all manner of difficulties to contend with. It would be naïve in the extreme to assume that we can tackle the challenges of grief in a 'painting by numbers' style. Rather, it is a matter of developing a substantial knowledge base, alongside our skills base, and being able to reflect critically on that knowledge base when we are in practice so that we can be helped by the insights it provides when we are wrestling with the complexities and nuances of loss and grief. That is, fundamentally, what critically reflective practice is all about, and so it is important that we understand that it is in this context that we need to address grief – thinking carefully and creatively about how best to proceed, with a professional knowledge base to draw upon, rather than looking for easy answers, magic solutions or simple procedures to follow.

The structure of the book

The book is divided into three parts, with each part containing three chapters. Part I is entitled 'Making Sense of Grief' and focuses on laying down a basic foundation of understanding so that we appreciate some of the key issues that we need to be aware of when we begin to help people deal with the challenges of grief. The first chapter explains some key terms and reviews some of the traditional theoretical models before providing an overview of some more recent developments in our thinking. The aim is to provide a sound foundation of understanding on which other chapters can then build.

Chapter 2 provides a discussion of crisis and trauma. It explains how crises – key turning points in people's lives – involve loss, often a range of losses, and are therefore very relevant when it comes to developing an understanding of grief. It also shows how loss and grief can bring about crises by putting so much pressure on people that they no longer feel able to cope. The chapter also explores how trauma, as a psychosocial wound, is also closely linked to issues of loss and grief. It explains how traumatic losses can be especially difficult to deal with, leaving us feeling ill-equipped to cope in the aftermath, when we feel devastated by the losses we have experienced – for example, as a result of being a victim of crime, abuse or violence.

Chapter 3 presents the key argument that, if we are to develop an adequate understanding of grief, then we need to see it in its social context. We need to see how grief does not operate in a vacuum. How people encounter loss, interpret grief and respond to it will all depend on a complex set of social factors. For example, we now know that gender is a significant variable when it comes to responding to loss (Doka and Martin, 2010), and we cannot therefore simply assume that everyone grieves in more or less the same way. Similarly, there are major cultural differences that we need to be aware of if we are not to rely on an oversimplified and far too narrow perspective on grief.

Part II is entitled 'Grief and Healing' and explores grief as a form of healing and, in doing so, helps us to understand what is happening when grief is following its normal course without any additional problems or complexities. Chapter 4 has the title 'Experiencing Grief' and serves to highlight the various ways in which people characteristically respond to loss. It shows that such responses will tend to fall into four categories: cognitive reactions (thought, concentration and memory); emotional reactions (feelings and moods); physical reactions (bodily responses); and spiritual reactions (questioning who we are and what our life is all about).

Chapter 5 is the first of two chapters that build on Chapter 4 by outlining some key issues that shape our response to loss – that is, our grief reactions. In this particular chapter the emphasis is on our *personal* responses, how the issues involved affect us at a personal level. It includes such important concepts as the universality of grief; emotional intelligence; and, perhaps most importantly of all, the need for self-care.

This is complemented by Chapter 6 where the focus is on our *professional* responses – that is, the various ways in which we can try to be a help and support to someone who is grieving, especially to someone who is struggling to cope with their grief even more than usual because of one or more complicating factors. This covers such important topics as 'being there' for people; assessing and managing risk; providing practical help; and contributing to healing in whatever ways we reasonably can.

Part III is entitled 'Grief without Healing'. In the three chapters here we concentrate on how grief can be problematic above and beyond the characteristic demands of a loss situation. We examine ways in which the healing of grieving can be blocked, interrupted or sidelined in some way. Chapter 7 explains what is meant by the technical term, 'complicated grief' and gives some examples of the types of situation that will generally be regarded as being indicative of complicated grief.

Chapter 8 follows on from this by providing some insights into the psychological problems that can be associated with grief. It highlights how stress, crisis and trauma; identity; inwardly directed emotions; and outwardly directed emotions can all be significant factors that can prove problematic in certain grief-related situations.

Chapter 9 complements this by exploring the relatively under-researched subject matter of how loss and grief contribute to *social* problems as well as the psychological ones covered in the previous chapter. It examines the significance of grief in relation to such social problems as: crime and imprisonment; abuse; social alienation and disaffection; violence; educational failure; family breakdown; and homelessness. It also shows how these problems, and the grief experiences that are intertwined with them, are interconnected in various ways.

Clearly, then, this is a book that covers a wide range of subject matter. My intention in adopting such a broad-based approach has been to map out how large and complex a terrain we are dealing with when we seek to tackle the challenges of grief. It is my hope that it will provide enough impetus to encourage you to go beyond the confines of this one book and keep learning about this vitally important aspect of what it means to be human.

A note about theory and practice

My work over the years has been characterized by a strong commitment to integrating theory and practice (Thompson, 2000; 2010; S. Thompson and N. Thompson, 2008). There is little value in a theory base that does not cast helpful light on the challenges of practice and considerable danger in practice that is not rooted in the understanding and insights that theory is intended to provide. I very much hope that the ideas presented in the book will be of benefit to practitioners wrestling with the immense difficulties involved, to students preparing for a career that involves addressing these difficulties and, of course, to grieving people who are seeking to make sense of what can often seem like the senseless situation they find themselves in.

The ideas on which the book is based are drawn from a very wide theoretical range – much wider than is generally the case in texts relating to grief – but what binds these ideas together into a coherent whole is a reliance on existentialist philosophy, an approach that emphasizes the significance of meaning, of the spiritual (or existential) challenges that we all face and the full recognition that to be human is to be mortal and to encounter many losses on our finite journey. To benefit from the insights this book offers it is not necessary to be familiar with existentialist ideas, but exploring what is involved in existentialism can help to broaden and deepen our understanding of grief and its challenges (see the 'Guide to further learning' at the end of the book).

PART I

Making sense of grief

Introduction

In a way, Part I of the book sets the scene for Parts II and III, where what is involved in helping people deal with grief is explored. Part I, then, is premised on the idea that it is important to understand grief to be able to deal with it, to respond to its many challenges. If not, we can make the experience worse or prolong the pain by dealing with matters without an adequate level of understanding of what is involved. There are, then, considerable dangers in terms of trying to help people deal with difficult and complex matters if we do not have at least a basic understanding of what is involved.

Part I is divided into three chapters. The first chapter, 'Loss and Grief', provides an overall view of loss (the event) and grief (the reaction to that loss). It covers a wide range of theoretical ideas, incorporating both traditional views of the subject and more recent theoretical developments that have begun to offer a more sophisticated understanding of what is involved in grief.

Chapter 2, 'Crisis and Trauma', explores the significance of crisis as a turning point in people's lives and draws links between the significance of crisis and the experience of grief. This chapter, as the chapter title implies, also provides an overview of trauma as a key factor in relation to grief. Trauma is a psychosocial (or 'existential') wound – that is, it refers to an experience that has wounded us in some way other than in the purely physical sense of a wound. The implications for this can be quite significant, as we shall see.

The third chapter, 'The Social Context', provides a good understanding of the various social phenomena that relate to grief. The traditional approach to grief is one that is primarily psychological, focusing in particular on the emotions involved in grief. This chapter will help us to realize that, while such issues are indeed very important, they are not the only ones. Grief occurs in a social context and is strongly influenced by that context, and so, once again, if we want to have an understanding of grief that does justice to the complexities involved, then we have to take account of the social (or, more specifically, sociological) aspects of grief.

1

Loss and grief

Introduction

This chapter sets the scene for the book by providing a basic introduction to the key terms and concepts and a summary of the main theoretical understandings that can cast light on this very complex and very sensitive set of issues. It challenges dominant notions that people grieve in stages or that there is one single, relatively standardized grieving process. It presents grieving as a set of processes that vary from individual to individual, across social groups and cultures and according to gender (these reflect themes that will be explored in more detail in Chapter 3). This chapter is also based on the idea that grief can arise in relation to any major loss and not just in response to a bereavement. This is an important point, as it is something that is often missed in the wider literature relating to loss which tends to focus primarily, if not exclusively at times, on death-related losses. Finally, this chapter introduces the notion of 'transformational' grief – that is, the kind of grief experience which, although painful, exhausting, frightening and confusing, can none the less have positive outcomes in terms of the grieving person growing and developing as a result of their painful and difficult experiences.

Key terms

In order to lay a foundation for understanding grief and its challenges it is important that we are clear about the terms we are using and what we mean by them. We therefore begin by clarifying some of the central concepts we need to understand to be able to develop a sound foundation on which to develop the knowledge base we need to do justice to the complexities involved.

In order to understand grief, we need to understand loss, and so 'loss' is the first key term that I shall be tackling. Of course, 'loss' is an everyday term that refers to having something and then no longer having it. But, when used more specifically in relation to grief, it refers to situations where we have something or someone who is important to us and then, for whatever reason, that person no longer features in our lives in the same way or that thing or entity that we value is now missing. So, loss is associated with a sense of emptiness. Where there was someone or something before, there is no longer, and this is one of the main reasons why such a strong sense of emptiness is so closely associated with loss and grief. Loss, then, is closely associated with another key term, namely 'cathexis'. 'Cathexis' is a psychological term that refers to an emotional investment. Freud used this term in his writings to refer to situations in which we form an attachment to someone or something. Because we have this emotional investment, it means that when we experience a loss, we then have a painful reaction because we have lost, in effect, our emotional investment. So what a person or thing means to us will be very significant (I shall return to the central role of meaning below). Cathexis is a helpful concept. It gives us an idea of why we can feel so devastated by a loss. It is the emotional equivalent of the Wall Street crash. That is, we put so much of ourselves into, for example, a relationship with a person, and when that person is no longer directly part of our lives – if they die, for example – then the net result can be one of a great sense that we have lost something of major value in our lives. This can lead to a great sense of insecurity.

Grief is, of course, itself a key term to be explained. It is often referred to as our emotional response to a loss, but this does not really tell the whole story. I prefer to see it as a holistic response to a loss and, by holistic, I mean a *biopsychosocial and spiritual* response. This is a complex notion, so it is important to break it down into its component parts:

- *Biological.*   There will be biological responses to a significant loss in our lives – for example, in terms of appetite, feeling unwell and so on.
- *Psychological.*   There will also be significant reactions at a psychological level, but we have to note that psychological does not mean simply emotional. Grief also affects us at a cognitive level, thereby, for example, making it difficult for us to concentrate, to think clearly or to remember. But even this is not the whole psychological picture. As well as cognitive and emotional (or 'affective', to use the technical term) aspects, there is the behavioural dimension of human psychology, so how we act and react will also be significant in response to a loss. Grief, then, is not simply an *emotional* response, but more broadly a *psychological* reaction and that, in itself, is only one part of this more holistic picture.
- *Social.*   This will be an important consideration in Chapter 3, where we explore the significance of such factors as social structure, culture and related sociological issues. The social dimension is particularly important for (at least) two main reasons: (i) all the other aspects of grief take place within a social context and are therefore to a large extent shaped by the range of factors that make up that context; and (ii) much of the existing literature on loss and grief pays little or no attention to the wider social context.
- *Spiritual.*   Loss can also be seen to have an impact on us at a spiritual level, whether our spirituality is of a religious kind or not. Spirituality is about such important matters as our frameworks of meaning, our sense of who we are and how we fit into the wider world – and all of these can be unsettled by the significance of grief in our lives at any particular moment.

Another key term associated with grief is that of 'bereavement'. Literally, to be bereaved means to be robbed, and that is a very significant term, as that is exactly how people tend to feel at the time of a major loss. In its literal sense, it does not necessarily mean a death-related loss, but it has come to refer to that in its everyday usage. So,

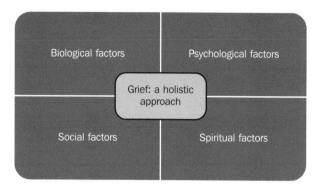

Figure 1.1 Grief: a holistic approach

when we talk about a bereavement, we are generally talking about a loss associated with a significant death. However, as we shall see as this book progresses, bereavement is indeed a major factor in relation to loss, but it is certainly not the only one. If we fall into the trap of automatically connecting issues of loss and grief with bereavement, then it is likely that we will fail to see just how significant other losses are in people's lives in general, and in the range of problems and issues addressed in the helping professions more specifically (Thompson, 2002). The following (not exhaustive) list of examples should help to highlight how pervasive loss experiences are:

- Accidents;
- Changing job;
- Divorce or relationship breakdown;
- Failure (an exam or job interview, for example);
- Loss of confidence;
- Loss of respect and credibility;
- Loss of self-respect (after an incident that causes shame);
- Miscarriage;
- Moving house;
- Natural disasters, like floods; and
- Still birth.

> PRACTICE FOCUS 1.1
>
> Kath was disappointed when she was told that, as part of the practice
> learning element of her degree programme, she would be working at a
> local hospice. She felt that this was outside the range of mainstream
> work that she wanted to work in when she completed her qualification.
> However, she was very pleasantly surprised to find that, not only did she
> learn a great deal about loss and grief in relation to terminal illness and
> palliative care, she also began to appreciate that loss and grief apply
> much more broadly and were, in reality, fundamental to what she
> regarded as 'mainstream' work. She was helped to understand that
> anyone, whatever their professional background or specific duties, who is
> working with people who are distressed, in need of care and/or support is
> likely to be encountering loss and grief issues in much of their work –
> even though many such professionals will not realize that this is the
> case. From this experience Kath had not only learned a great deal, but
> had also been fired with enthusiasm to make sure she would not make
> the mistake of failing to recognize the significance of losses in people's
> lives that were not specifically death related.

The final key term I want to explore is that of 'mourning'. This
refers to the way grief is experienced collectively rather than individually, so one way of looking at it is that an individual *grieves* while a
community *mourns*. So, when we are looking at mourning, we tend
to be concerned with such matters as rituals and other established
patterns of groups of people, whether communities in the sense of a
neighbourhood or the broader sense of a community of interest (for
example, a set of colleagues in a workplace). What we are dealing
with is the way a community collectively responds to an experience
of loss and grief. This is important because it emphasizes the social
dimensions of loss and grief that are so often neglected, with the
tendency to focus primarily (or even at times exclusively) on psychological aspects.

Traditional theories of grief

Having explored some key terms that will help to provide some
degree of understanding of grief, let us now move on to look at how

some people have tried to explain grief in terms of a particular theoretical approach. Perhaps the best known and most well established of these is what has come to be known as the stages approach, which is associated with such writers as Elizabeth Kübler-Ross (1969). This theory has had a profound and far-reaching influence. In fact, it is quite significant to note just how influential it has been, considering how, in general, social science theories are, for the most part, not widely known in the minds of the general public.

It is therefore unfortunate that this theory has now largely been discredited as, despite this, it continues to be one that is widely used and widely talked about. The basic idea behind the theory is that, when we are grieving, we go through a set of stages; we follow a particular pattern. These stages are deemed to be:

- *Denial.* This refers to the sense of unreality that often arises when we come face to face with a major loss experience – the sense of 'No, it can't be. There must be a mistake.' It can take us quite a while to work through this sense of unreality. It is as if our head knows that we have experienced a major loss, but our heart takes a while to catch up, for the idea to 'sink in' at an emotional level.
- *Anger.* This relates to situations where the intense feelings generated by the loss are directed outwards towards other people as anger or resentment. As we shall see in Chapter 4, such feelings can also be directed inwards as a strong sense of irrational guilt.
- *Bargaining.* Faced with significant changes brought about by loss, we may begin to negotiate, to enter into a process of bargaining.
- *Depression.* A sense of hopelessness and helplessness can lead to a depressed frame of mind and mood, a psychological state characterized by lethargy, low motivation, pessimism and negativity.
- *Acceptance.* This refers to the presumed end point of grief, the stage where we have 'come to terms' with our loss.

Despite the influence of this approach, it has now been challenged from various quarters. The basic thrust of the counter-argument is that there is little or no research evidence (or for that matter clinical or practice evidence) to support the idea that people grieve in this linear stage by stage way (Neimeyer, 2001a). Attig (2011) also warns of the dangers of relying on a stages model of grief, as does Bonanno (2009), Harvey (2002) and Walter (1994). Neimeyer (2000) captures the point well when he argues that:

Much of what we know about the human response to loss derives from studies of adults who have lost a loved one through death. At least in the cases of profound and irretrievable loss, there appear to be certain common reactions, feelings and processes of healing for those who are bereaved, although there are also important variations among mourners as a result of who they are, how they typically cope with adversity, and the nature of their relationship to the deceased individual. For this reason, it is misleading to speak of 'stages' of grieving, as if all mourners follow the same path in their journey from painful separation to personal restoration. (p. 5)

Voice of experience 1.1

❝I was taught the stages approach at college, but in practice the people I was working with didn't seem to fall into that pattern. For me it seemed too neat and tidy, while what I was constantly coming across in my practice was much messier, much more chaotic – and much more variable from person to person. The idea of stages just didn't fit with the situations I was coming across.**❞**

Lynn, a counsellor based at a GP surgery

However, there is evidence to suggest that people *try* to grieve in stages, strongly suggesting that this model has become a prescriptive one, rather than a descriptive or explanatory one. For example, the work of Walter (1994) has indicated that the theory has become so well established, especially in the United States, that it is taken as read that this is how people will grieve. This is reflected in popular literature, TV drama and cinema where uncritical references to grieving in stages are fairly commonplace. In addition, the philosopher, Žižek, has written a book about what he sees as the end of capitalism and has structured it around Kübler-Ross's five stages (Žižek, 2010).

Following the initial critique of the stages model, many people tried to salvage it by proposing that it should not be taken too literally that the stages occur in a set order. It was therefore suggested that these stages may be experienced in a different order and in different ways by different people. However, there are two problems with this approach. First of all, if the 'stages' do not occur in a set order, then of course they are not stages. It is nonsensical to refer to aspects of a situation that do not occur in a specific order as stages. Second, there is a great deal of evidence to show that, even if we disregard the idea of linearity to the stages, then it is still not correct to assume that everyone experiences these stages. For example, one of the stages is depression. The work of Schneider (2000) has argued strongly and convincingly that there is a great danger in mistaking grief for depression, and so what we will note is that very many people will grieve in ways that do not include depression (Schneider, 2006), but which superficially may appear like depression:

> Grief is a normal, healthy, healing and ultimately transforming response to a significant loss that usually does not require professional help, although it does require finding ways to heal the broken strands of life and to affirm existing ones. … Depression, on the other hand, represents a state of disconnection that can be the result of a biological, psychological, spiritual, or even circumstantial imbalance that makes it impossible to function fully after a loss. You begin to just exist, and, in the extreme, only are alive until death itself provides the release. Depression is the inability to grieve, either temporarily or permanently. (p. 26)

I would also want to add to this the idea of bargaining. For example, in my own work over very many years, I have encountered many people who, in their grieving, do indeed undertake a certain amount of bargaining or negotiation. For example, they may express a commitment to being a better person in the hope that this will some-how reduce the pain they are experiencing. However, I have also worked with a large number of people where this does not feature at all in how they manage and experience their grieving. We therefore have to recognize that the basic idea that people grieve in stages is highly problematic as a theoretical basis for understanding – despite the fact that it is such a widely held, and sometimes even cherished, theoretical understanding of grief.

So, if grief is not simply a matter of people going through a set of stages, how can we explain what happens in grief? There are various ways of doing this. One of them is what has come to be known as the 'tasks approach' to grieving. This is linked to the idea of develop-mental psychology whereby, in growing and developing over time, we face certain developmental tasks. For example, an adolescent faces the developmental task of making the transition from childhood to adulthood. So, it is in this sense that the term 'tasks' is being used. The work of William Worden in this regard has been very helpful and influential. It has established a better understanding of what happens when someone is grieving than the simplistic reliance on the stages model (Worden, 2009). Worden's tasks can be described as follows:

1. *Accepting the reality of the loss.*   Getting used to the idea that the person (or thing) is no longer physically with us.
2. *Working through the pain of grief.*   Dealing, as far as possible, with the pain involved in the loss.
3. *Adjusting to a changed environment, externally, internally and spiritually.*   Getting used to the wider changes brought about by the loss.
4. *Emotionally relocating the deceased and moving on with life.* This means continuing to have a meaningful, loving relation-ship with the deceased, but in a new context.

This has proven to be a helpful model that has cast a lot of light on the complexities of grieving. However, it can be argued that it is not enough on its own, that it needs to be supplemented by other forms of understanding. For example, while there is some support for the idea of developmental stages, this in itself does not explain the complexities of how different individuals grieve in different ways or, indeed, how the social context plays an important role.

As originally described by Worden (in the 1983 edition of his book), the fourth task was characterized as 'withdrawing emotional energy from the deceased and reinvesting it in another relationship'. This idea of 'letting go' and moving on after grief has been challenged by the work of Klass, Silverman and Nickman (1996) in terms of what has come to be known as the 'continuing bonds thesis'. Behind this idea is research which strongly suggests that people may benefit from continuing their relationship with the deceased person and, in effect, transforming that relationship, rather than relinquishing it. As Attig (2011) puts it:

> We need not break our bonds with the deceased but instead redefine those bonds and their places in our lives. Rather than challenging us to separate from the dead, their deaths challenge us to maintain meaningful connection and to integrate redefined relationships in our necessarily new life patterns. (p. 174)

Worden's later work has supported this idea, and so its reformulation in the 1991 edition was quite significant.

One further attempt to go beyond the stages model is that associated with Therese Rando who developed what is known as the 'Six Rs' approach (Rando, 1993). She writes about six tasks that need to be achieved when a person is grieving. DeSpelder and Strickland (2005) summarize the approach as follows:

1. Recognize the loss (acknowledge and understand the death).
2. React to the separation (experience the pain; feel, identify, accept, and express the reactions to the loss; and identify and mourn the secondary losses).
3. Recollect and re-experience the deceased and the relationship (review and remember realistically; revive and re-experience the feelings).

4. Relinquish the old attachments to the deceased and the old assumptive world.
5. Readjust to move adaptively into the new world without forgetting the old (develop a new relationship with the deceased , adopt new ways of being in the world, form a new identity).
6. Reinvest. (p. 284)

This is another theoretical approach that has taken forward our understanding in a number of ways but which also is not enough on its own. For example, it also has relatively little to say about the complexities of the social context in which grieving takes place. In addition, once again the notion of 'relinquishing old attachments' raises questions about whether this approach is sophisticated enough to take account of the significance of 'continuing bonds'.

So, while it is an important contribution to our understanding, it still leaves much unexplained and therefore room for other theoretical perspectives to supplement and complement the insights provided by Rando's work.

PRACTICE FOCUS 1.2

Kevin had applied to go on the training course on loss and grief a few months before the actual day of the event and, at the time, he had not thought that, on the day of the course, he would be wrestling with his own grief issues. Kevin's brother died three weeks before the course, and so he was faced with a major decision: should he withdraw from the course because it would be too painful for him, too 'close to home', or should he see it through to see whether it would help him deal with his own issues. In the end, he decided to attend and, while it proved to be very difficult for him in some ways (and at times during the day, he was wishing he had not attended), one thing made it very worthwhile for him. He learned about the idea of 'continuing bonds' and this made him feel a lot more at ease about the loss of his brother. He realized that, while he would no longer have any physical contact with his brother, he would always be an important part of his life, always part of his sense of who he was. This notion of 'continuing bonds' was therefore one that Kevin took a lot of comfort from.

A further traditional perspective on loss is to be found in attachment theory. Associated originally with the work of Bowlby (1981), it has proven to be an influential approach in relation to child development theory and childcare practice. It is based on the idea that children develop an emotional attachment to a primary caregiver (the mother in the original formulation of the theory). Such attachments, it is argued, influence how we think about the world. Eliason, Lepore and Myer (2008) explain Bowlby's approach in the following terms:

> He uses the belief that the foundation of individuals' relationships stems from the early attachment between individuals and their caregivers. By incorporating a unique cognitive component in his model, Bowlby suggests that cognitive biases influence personal perceptions and belief systems. The concept is based on individuals' experience of attachment, and the later separation anxiety that children experience with maturity and the absence of their caregivers. Separation anxiety is a response to the threat of loss, and bereavement is a reaction to the loss. Subsequent losses and relationships are influenced and processed by cognitive biases formed early in life evoking similar emotions. (p. 420)

Attachment theory therefore helps us to understand that how we respond to losses in our adult life will depend on our early life experiences of attachment, separation and loss.

This is not a comprehensive overview of traditional theories of grief, but it should be sufficient to give a flavour of the types of ideas that have been used to try and make sense of grief and associated phenomena. Each of them has something to offer in terms of developing understanding. Even the highly criticized stages approach casts some light on what happens when people grieve. For example, if we think of the stages as aspects of grief, rather than steps in a process, and, if we move away from the idea that there is a standard or standardized approach to grieving, then there is some degree of understanding to be offered by this traditional perspective. So overall, what we have from the traditional theory base is a set of ideas which make some degree of contribution to our understanding of grief, but which still leave much more to be said. That, then, brings us to contemporary theories of grief which have taken our understanding a great deal further but which, of course, still leave much unexplained, as it would be idealistic to expect a theory (or even a set of theories) to provide all the understanding that is needed. Having reviewed some of the traditional approaches to making sense of the complexities of loss, let us now move on to look at more recent theories of grief.

Contemporary theories of grief

As with the traditional theories of loss, there are various theories that come under this heading, and it would not be realistic for me to attempt to provide an exhaustive account of these. I am therefore going to focus on three theories in particular: dual process theory; meaning reconstruction; and transformational grief.

A key development in our understanding of grief has been the idea of the dual process model of grief. This derives from the work of Stroebe and Schut, based in the Netherlands, who have provided a very helpful and insightful model of grief that is based on two co-existing processes (hence the term, *dual* process). Stroebe and Schut (1999) write about a 'loss orientation' to grief and this process refers to the way we look back on who or what we have lost and reflect on the significance of that loss. It is therefore characterized by sadness, anger and so on. But, there is also 'restoration orientation' to be considered. This refers to the process of looking forward, of thinking about how life will be different now without the person or thing that has been lost, looking towards developing in a sense a new identity, a new approach to life based on the new transformed circumstances.

What Stroebe and Schut put forward by way of a theoretical construct is the notion that we 'oscillate' between these two orientations when we are grieving. That is, a grieving person may be in loss orientation in the morning but, by the afternoon, may have moved to restoration orientation and back to loss orientation in the evening.

The basic idea is that, over time, the grieving individual will spend less time in loss orientation and more time in restoration orientation but will, none the less, continue to oscillate between the two. For example, even years after a significant loss, when restoration orientation has been very strongly to the fore, if the person concerned is reminded of their loss, then for a few minutes, hours, days or even weeks, they may be back in loss orientation temporarily before they return to restoration orientation.

Voice of experience 1.2

"One of my clients summed it up perfectly. She said that, when she lost her husband, it was like a roller-coaster ride. She would start to go up, then plummet down again, and it went on like that for quite some time.**"**

Paul, a community psychiatric nurse

We can see that this theory offers a much more dynamic understanding of grief and reflects more fully the moving, changing nature of grief, as compared with the traditional models which do not capture that same sense of a dynamic, changing picture. Dual process theory is also helpful in establishing the idea that different people will grieve in different ways because, for example, each individual will oscillate at a different rate at different times. So, in many ways, this approach can be seen as a significant step forward in terms of developing our understanding.

However, this is not the only development in loss theory. Another very significant step forward has come from the work of Neimeyer and his colleagues in the United States who have developed what has come to be known as meaning reconstruction theory (Neimeyer, 2001a, b; Neimeyer and Anderson, 2002). What this refers to is the idea that, when we lose someone (or something) very close to us, then we lose not only that person (or thing), but also what they meant to us. We then face the difficult and painful process of constructing a new meaning without the person (or thing) we have lost.

A key concept within meaning reconstruction theory is narrative: the idea of a story that helps us to make sense of our lives. So, in effect, what we are doing when we are grieving, according to this theory, is we are rewriting the story of our life. We are in a sense moving on to a new chapter in terms of what our life now means to us. In this way, what is happening is that we are developing new meanings that allow us to retain a relationship with the person (or thing) we have lost, but which recognizes that that relationship is a very different one as a result of the loss that has occurred – it has been transformed rather than destroyed. As Hedtke and Winslade (2004) put it: 'If we are shaped by stories as much as by realities, then it is also possible for us to shape our experience differently through telling the story differently' (p. 41).

This, too, has proven to be an influential theory and is now widely quoted in the academic literature and widely used in professional practice. It involves looking at grief from the point of view of the individual concerned in terms of what it means to them within their unique frame of reference, within their unique universe of meaning. It is therefore far removed from the idea of each person going through a set of fairly standardized stages. One of the main advantages of this theory is that it very clearly shows that different people grieve in different ways. It therefore moves completely away from the simplistic notion that grief is a standardized process that happens to everybody in more or less the same way.

One further key development in terms of our understanding of grief has come from work which is focused on the idea of transformational grief (Calhoun and Tedeschi, 2001; Schneider, 2006). This refers to the recognition that, while grief can be an extremely painful and difficult process, it is not necessarily entirely negative. Grief can lead to significant changes in a person's life which turn out to be very positive. For example, someone who has experienced a major loss may, as a result of that loss, review their life and then engage with their various life challenges in a new and more effective way. For example, I have come across people who have acknowledged that, prior to a significant loss, they were not making anything of their life; they had friends and relatives they did not appreciate; they were allowing their life to be wasted in a sense, but, following a significant loss, they changed that approach: they now appreciate who and what they have by way of an important life environment, and they are determined to make the most of the life they have. This is a classic example of transformational grief, the recognition that grief is not something that we should just help people to 'get over'. It is something that can have a silver lining.

From a professional helper point of view, this is very significant, as it means that, without a knowledge of transformational grief, we may miss significant opportunities to help people grow and develop as a result of their significant loss. This is closely linked to the idea of crisis intervention and also to the notion of post-traumatic growth, important topics we will return to in Chapter 2.

PRACTICE FOCUS 1.3

Larry was a quiet, withdrawn and fairly unconfident individual with few friends and no real interests to speak of. He worked as a porter in a local hospital. He was reasonably happy with his lot for the most part, but was prone to depression from time to time. However, all this changed one day when, while Larry was working with two colleagues removing some boxes that had been dumped in the hospital parking lot, two youths in a stolen car raced through at high speed. Larry managed to jump out of the way but his two colleagues did not – they were killed instantly right in front of his eyes. He was quite shocked by this and found the intense feelings the incident generated extremely hard to deal with in the coming weeks and months. There were times when he wondered whether he might 'crack up' as he could not get the incident out of his mind.

Over time, though, he managed to recover from the trauma with the help of a social worker. He was able to start to get things into proportion. However, he was also able to go beyond this. Seeing two young men killed instantly had made him review his life and consider carefully what he wanted out of it and where he wanted it to take him. As a result of this he decided to attend night classes to gain the entry qualifications that would allow him to commence nurse training. After realizing how fragile life can be, he now had a clear sense of wanting to do something positive with his life rather than just let it drift past. The trauma had turned out to be a point of growth for him – an intensely painful experience, but one that ultimately brought important positive benefits.

(Thompson, 2009a)

These, then, are just some of the key developments in grief theory that have added an extra layer of understanding to that offered by the traditional long-standing theories. As I mentioned earlier, this does not mean that we have now arrived at a point where we have a more or less complete understanding of grief, but we have certainly moved forward in significant ways, and we now have better tools for addressing the complexities by recognizing more fully the dynamic nature of grief, the diversity associated with grief (that is, the recognition that different people grieve in different ways) and the complexities of grief.

Breadth and depth

One last aspect of understanding of grief that I wish to explore in this chapter is the question of breadth and depth. This is because I have concerns about how both these dimensions have a tendency to be neglected much of the time (albeit, thankfully, not all of the time – there are some notable exceptions) so, before leaving the subject, I want to take the opportunity to emphasize the importance of taking account of both the breadth and depth of grief.

Breadth

By 'breadth' of grief I mean two things:

1. As already noted, grief issues tend to be conceptualized predominantly in individualistic, psychological terms. Such a narrow focus then has the effect of neglecting wider social and spiritual concerns, thereby presenting a distorted picture of grief. Such a distortion is dangerous because it means that people who are grieving will not have the full picture relating to what they are going through and may therefore focus too narrowly on, say, emotional issues (Hockey, 1996), while paying little or no attention to the help, solace and nurturance that can be gained from connecting with the wider social picture and the spiritual realm. We shall return to these issues in later chapters.

2. As also already noted, grief tends to be mainly associated with death-related losses, with relatively little attention given to other forms of loss. In reality, loss (and therefore grief) is much more widespread than is generally realized. Figure 1.2 gives an overview of the wide range of losses that tend to feature in people's lives, but even this is not exhaustive. It is therefore important that we get the balance right. On the one hand, we must not lose sight of how important bereavement is and how strong and devastating an effect it can have on individuals, families and whole communities, while also recognizing that death-related losses form only one part of a much broader

---

What can be lost

A relationship (divorce or relationship breakdown)
One or more abilities (for example, through accident, illness or disability)
Faith (religious, political or whatever)
A sense of self-worth (through shame)
Confidence and self-esteem (as a result of being bullied, for example)
Status or authority (as a result of changes at work perhaps)

How loss can occur

Traumatic losses
- Being a victim of crime
- Being a victim of violence
- Being abused

Developmental transitions
- Adolescence
- A child growing up and leaving home
- Retiring from work

Redundancy / layoff
Being discriminated against
A child being removed from their family for their own safety or welfare
An elderly person moving permanently into a residential home
Having to abandon a cherished plan, project or ambition
Being imprisoned
Being the parent, partner, child, close relative or friend of someone who is imprisoned

---

Figure 1.2 The range of losses and loss experiences

picture of loss and grief in human life. Our perspective therefore needs to be broad enough to take account of both death-
related losses and those losses that are not directly linked to
bereavement.

Depth

As with the breadth of grief, in emphasizing the importance of depth
in relation to grief, there are two aspects to focus on:

1. Depth can refer to the intensity associated with grief. I cannot
   overemphasize just how intense and painful the impact of grief
   can be (whether death related or not). Professional helpers
   need to be very careful not to lose sight of just how crushing
   the pressures of grief can be. Whenever we are working with
   people who are grieving, we therefore need to ensure that we
   keep a clear focus on how intense a landscape of suffering
   grief occupies.
2. We can also understand depth to mean complexity – that is,
   deep as opposed to superficial and thus oversimplified. Grief
   is complex because:

   (a) It has different dimensions (biological, psychological,
       social and spiritual);
   (b) Different people grieve in different ways(due to a combi-
       nation of personal, situational and social factors);
   (c) How one person is grieving can affect how another person
       is grieving (and individuals and groups can influence each
       other);
   (d) Grief can become problematic (or 'complicated') in vari-
       ous ways – see Chapter 7 – and can also contribute to
       personal and social problems (see Chapters 8 and 9
       respectively);
   (e) Common sense understandings of grief can be very
       misleading (for example, the idea that people grieve in
       stages or that grief is a form of illness or pathology);

(f) As noted earlier, there is a wide range of situations that can produce a grief reaction, not just when a bereavement occurs.

Voice of experience 1.3

"Working on a geriatric ward has helped me realize just how much grief features in older people's lives. I think I was naïve at first and hadn't understood that losses could make such a difference to people's lives."

Debbie, a nurse in a general hospital

Clearly, then, grief is a phenomenon that needs to be understood in relation to both breadth and depth if we are to avoid oversimplifying it and presenting a distorted picture of what is involved. The chapters that follow should make a good contribution to appreciating both the breadth and the depth.

Conclusion

What this chapter has tried to show is that there are various ways of trying to understand loss and grief, various theoretical perspectives, none of which offers a definitive overview but which in combination provide the beginnings of an excellent platform for developing our knowledge further. This is based on the idea that, as mentioned in the Introduction, there is a need for a good understanding of loss and grief if we are to be well equipped to help people cope with the challenges involved.

It is to be hoped that what this chapter has also shown is that grief is broader than people generally think, that it is not simply something which applies when someone dies, as there are a whole range of losses in people's lives that can have a significant impact on how they engage with other people and engage with their life challenges in general. We have also seen that grief is more complex than people generally think, that there is far more to it than the simplistic understandings that have come to be established over the decades.

In this way, the chapter has created a foundation from which we can build a fuller understanding. We will now take that understanding a step further by looking at the significance of crisis and trauma as key factors linked to loss and grief. These will be the subject matter of Chapter 2.

POINTS TO PONDER

- Why do you think it is important to have a theoretical understanding of grief?
- How might the idea of 'transformational grief' be of use in practice?
- Why is it important to have a broad view of grief?

Key texts

1. Corr, C. A., Nabe, C. M. and Corr, D. M. (2008) *Death & Dying, Life & Living*, 6th edn, Belmont, CA, Thomson Higher Education.
2. DeSpelder, L. A. and Strickland, A. L. (2005) *The Last Dance: Encountering Death and Dying*, 7th edition, London, McGraw-Hill Higher Education.
3. Dickenson, D., Johnson, M. and Katz, J. S. (eds) (2000) *Death, Dying and Bereavement*, London, Sage.

2

Crisis and trauma

Introduction

In this chapter, we focus on how crisis points in people's lives and the experience of psychological trauma can produce significant grief reactions that can have lasting effects. It presents theoretical understandings of crisis and trauma, as well as a discussion of the practice implications of working with people who are exposed to such challenging life experiences. The chapter shows how demanding such work can be and warns of the dangers of trying to come up with simplistic solutions to what are in reality very complex problems. It also offers a warning about the dangers of adopting a medicalized approach to what are fundamentally psychosocial issues. The significance of this will become apparent in the pages that follow.

Crisis

In everyday speech, crisis is used in at least two main ways. It can mean a turning point in somebody's life; a critical moment where things will either get better or get worse, but they will not stay the same. It can also be used in the sense of an emergency, 'crisis' being used as a term to mean a situation characterized by urgency, one that has to be dealt with very, very soon if things are not to get considerably worse. It is important to note that the way the term crisis is used in the professional literature underpinning the helping professions refers to the former and not to the latter. That is, what we are looking at is the idea of crisis as a turning point, rather than necessarily an urgent situation:

A crisis is defined as a turning point in someone's life, a critical moment where the situation will either get better or get worse, but it will (by definition) not stay the same. The term is commonly confused with an emergency, a situation that needs to be addressed urgently. However, while the two terms, 'crisis' and 'emergency' can overlap at times, it is important to recognize the significance between them. ... Many emergencies are not crises at all, in the sense that they do not involve a person's coping resources being overwhelmed or amount to a 'turning point' situation. They may well become a crisis if they are not attended to urgently, and so they may be seen as potential crisis points, rather than necessarily actual crisis moments. (N. Thompson and S. Thompson, 2008, pp. 247–8)

A crisis involves a breakdown of what is known as 'homeostasis'. This is parallel with 'thermostasis' – that is, the regulation of heat in a central heating system controlled by a thermostatic valve (the thermostat). In the same way that a central heating system has a temperature within a certain range, from the lowest point to the highest point, but broadly around the same temperature level. That is how a thermostat works. It switches off when the highest point is reached and switches back on again when the lowest one is reached, with the result that it keeps the temperature within an acceptable range. The idea of homeostasis is very similar to this. It relates to how people cope with their everyday demands and challenges. What tends to happen is that we will manage to cope better on some days than others, but will tend to stay within our normal range. Although at times our coping ability will be higher than at others, and will sometimes be relatively low, it will generally stay within our characteristic range – we will maintain 'homeostasis'.

A crisis, then, is a situation when that homeostasis breaks down, when it takes us outside of our normal range of coping, where we feel we can no longer deal with the situation through our normal mechanisms. Of course, many loss situations are crisis situations (see, for example, McBride and Johnson, 2005; O'Halloran, Ingala and Copeland, 2005). If somebody has experienced a major bereavement, for example, then there is a strong possibility that this will plunge them into a crisis by taking them beyond their normal range of coping abilities. In this way, crisis is associated with *problems*, with situations that we find very difficult to cope with because they require coping resources above and beyond those that are at our disposal. It requires us to find new ways of coping, new problem-solving approaches that will enable us to return to the relative comfort and security of homeostasis.

However, there is also a positive side to such situations. A crisis is also a potential point of growth. Because a point has been reached that goes beyond homeostasis, then new ways of coping have to be found. This can mean that the person in crisis can really struggle to find a way forward but, when they do, that way forward can help them significantly in terms of their own lives.

Another important aspect of crisis is the distinction between an anticipated crisis and an unexpected one. An anticipated crisis is one where we can predict that a crisis point will be reached – for example, when we know that somebody is retiring and will need to adapt to new circumstances. In this way, the turning point can be planned for and can be managed, with little or no distress involved. This is what distinguishes crisis in this professional sense from the everyday usage of meaning an emergency. However, other types of crisis can be unexpected: they occur without any warning sign. This can be, for example, as a result of a death or other significant loss that affects us. In such circumstances, there is little or no opportu-nity to plan for what has happened and, because we have been caught unawares, the crisis is likely to be far more difficult to deal with.

Whichever type of crisis arises, the aim for the professional helper remains the same – that is, to enhance coping, to help the individual or individuals concerned to learn from the experience, to develop better coping mechanisms for when they encounter such challenging experiences again in future. In this respect, being involved in a crisis (crisis intervention, to use the technical term) can be seen as a form of empowerment (Thompson, 2007, 2011a). It is a way of helping people to address their own problems in their own ways. Very often when someone is in crisis, they feel overwhelmed by what they are facing, and this can often result in a form of paralysis where the person concerned feels unable to move forward; they feel stuck. The involvement of a professional helper can therefore be crucial in helping them to move forward positively.

However, as we shall note in relation to loss situations in general in Chapter 6, we should not assume that, just because someone is in crisis, professional help is needed. The majority of crises that people experience will be managed either alone or with the informal support of the people in their own everyday support networks. Professional help should be offered only in those circumstances where it is needed (which should be part of the professional assessment carried out when we encounter a person in crisis). Being in crisis is not, in itself, a reason for professional involvement, just as experiencing grief is not sufficient in itself to warrant professional intervention.

Voice of experience 2.1

“When I first started in this job, whenever I came across somebody who was having a crisis I wanted to get a whole army of professionals involved. Thankfully I had a very experienced and supportive boss who helped me to understand that we should only refer on if we had reason to believe that people weren't getting enough support from within their own network of family, friends and community supports.”

Ros, a community development worker

Crisis scenarios have significant echoes of grief situations where, in those circumstances where professional help is needed, the professional helper can again potentially play a key role in helping somebody who is stuck to move forward. We will explore these issues in more depth in Chapter 7. However, for now it is important to recognize that there is a two-way relationship between grief and crisis. In one direction, a crisis can provoke a grief reaction. Because it is a turning point in somebody's life, it involves a degree of change or transition, and therefore there are elements of loss involved. Consequently, somebody who is in crisis can encounter the significant challenges of grief.

PRACTICE FOCUS 2.1

Zafar had been in his current post for almost three years and had always found it difficult right from the start. He had hoped that things would get easier over time, but that proved not to be the case. The situation had the effect of undermining his confidence, with the result that he felt trapped in a job he was struggling with, but he did not have the self-belief to apply for a job that was more suited to his abilities. However, matters came to a head when his girlfriend left him. She said she could no longer face being with him because he was so miserable most of the time. Zafar was devastated by this and felt he could no longer go on. The quality of his work fell drastically and he started neglecting himself, including his personal hygiene. It quickly reached the point where his supervisor took him on one side and told him that, if he did not get back to normal pretty soon, he would face disciplinary proceedings and the likelihood of dismissal. Zafar felt dreadful and did not know where to turn. After years of being quite settled, albeit not particularly happy, he now found his life had been turned upside down. He was in danger of losing his job and, unless he made some significant changes, he stood very little chance of getting his girlfriend back. Realizing this made him feel even worse and he could feel himself slipping into a spiral, a vicious circle of negativity. All this changed, however, when his brother called round to see him and was amazed to find him in such a desperate state. Talking to his brother about what had gone wrong in his life was the spur that Zafar needed, the turning point that enabled him to begin to feel motivated to turn things round. His brother helped him understand that the root of his problems had been his acceptance of a job that he was not happy in. He realized now that, if he was to get out of this spiral, he would have to get a different job. He cleaned himself up and set about trying to do something positive about his work situation. This small but significant change gave him the boost he needed to make the changes to his life that were called for. He had hit rock bottom and was now on the way up. The crisis really was a turning point for him that could now lead to a much happier situation than the one he was in before the crisis.

This can happen in the opposite direction too, where loss can provoke a crisis. That is, because of a major loss experienced, the person concerned can find that they no longer cope. Imagine, for example, somebody losing their long-time life partner and then feeling that their life has been changed so much that they become convinced that they cannot go on, that something has to change (see Practice focus 2.1).

Because of this two-way relationship, there is the potential for a vicious circle to emerge. That is, a crisis can provoke a grief reaction; the grief reaction can provoke a further crisis; and the further crisis can then lead to more grief, and so on, leading into a destructive spiral in which the individual at the heart of it is overwhelmed by wave after wave of grief. It is therefore very important for professionals dealing with people in crisis to be aware of this potential for a vicious circle and to try and prevent it where possible.

When we are working with people in crisis we therefore have to look at what grief issues are at play in the situation. It does not follow automatically that grief will feature but, in my experience, it does so in a high proportion of cases, although this can be easily missed if we are not tuned in to the very significant links between grief and crisis. That is, if we are not actively aware of the fact that crises often involve grief, then at best we will fail to do the utmost we can to help people in difficult circumstances, and at worst we could make the situation even more distressing by insensitively walking all over their feelings – perhaps unwittingly giving a powerful message that we lack understanding and sensitivity and that we are therefore not to be trusted as helpers. When someone is feeling vulnerable, they may well be very wary about who they trust, so such insensitivity on our part may be sufficient to lead to their refusing help from us.

It can also work the other way around, in the sense that, if we are working with somebody who is grieving, we will need to ask ourselves whether that person is in crisis: Are they coping with the pain and suffering involved in a way that is part of their normal coping mechanisms, or have they reached the point where their coping resources are being overwhelmed? This is an important question because, if we fail to recognize the significance of crisis for some people who are grieving, then we will not have an accurate picture of the situation that we are trying to deal with. This can leave us ill-equipped to help.

PRACTICE FOCUS 2.2

Anita was a staff development officer who had been invited to give a talk about crisis intervention to a group of volunteers for a local mental health voluntary organization. In her talk she described how one crisis can lead to another and to another, leaving the individual concerned at a loss as to how to go on. She put forward the idea that the net result of this can be someone experiencing significant mental health problems, even where they have no previous history of such problems. After her talk Anita was chatting to a few of the volunteers when one of them asked if he could have a word with her in private. He wanted to let her know that he had found her talk helpful as what she described was what had happened to him. His son had been killed in a car crash. He grieved so intensely that he lost sight of the small business he was running, resulting in the business failing. He then became quite depressed and soon afterwards his wife left him, as she was looking to him for support in mourning their son's loss but was not getting any. The next step was that he could not pay the mortgage and he subsequently became homeless. He then had what he described as a 'mental breakdown'. He received a great deal of help from the voluntary body that was hosting the event at which Anita was speaking. Once he was back on his feet again he decided to 'repay his debts' by acting as a volunteer. Anita was saddened to hear of his tragic story, but was pleased to hear that he had found her talk helpful.

Voice of experience 2.2

❝In my job I encounter a lot of grief. Generally people just cope as best they can, with the help of relatives – and our carers, of course – but sometimes, we can see that the resident is not coping and we have to consider what steps we have to take to help them through their crisis.❞

Andrea, manager of a nursing home

These questions, then, relating to the relationship between grief and crisis can be seen to have significant implications for practice and therefore need to be considered very carefully. Both grief and crisis can be extremely difficult, demanding and painful experiences to go through, but they also have the potential for growth and transformation. Strange though it may seem, given the immense vulnerability associated with both grief and crisis, there really is significant potential for people to emerge stronger and better equipped to deal with the challenges they will face in the future. From suffering and vulnerability come strength and empowerment. Indeed, Brandon (2000) equates vulnerability with strength, and there is a long-standing idea of suffering producing strength and learning (it was, for example, a key feature of the philosophy of Friedrich Nietzsche, one of the most influential writers and thinkers ever – see Wicks, 2002). Vulnerability, suffering, strength and learning are all key parts of what it means to be human. We shall return to this theme later in this chapter when we discuss the notion of 'post-traumatic growth'.

Trauma

The term 'trauma' is used in the medical profession to refer to a wound, but it is also used in the helping profession more broadly to refer to what is often known as a psychological wound. In reality, however, a trauma is more than psychological, it is more specifically a psychosocial and spiritual phenomenon. It can even be described as an existential wound (Thompson and Walsh, 2010), in the sense that it has a profound impact on our sense of self and our understanding of the world (Harvey, 2002, describes trauma as an 'assault on the self'). It is worth exploring each of these different elements in terms of trauma and its significance:

- *Psychological*. A trauma can affect all three dimensions of human psychology – that is, thoughts, feelings and actions. At the thoughts or cognitive level, a trauma can make it difficult for people to focus and to think clearly. This can be quite distressing in many situations. There are also emotional factors to take into account, in the sense that a trauma can be profoundly upsetting, leading to a wide range of emotional responses. This is largely because trauma, as we shall see below, is closely linked to grief, and so the emotional reactions associated with grief can also be seen to apply to trauma. Similar comments can be made about the behavioural dimension of psychology: people who are going (or have gone) through a trauma can behave in uncharacteristic ways – in fact, quite bizarrely at times.

- *Social*. There is also a social dimension, in the sense that, when somebody experiences a trauma, how they react to it will be partly influenced by their culture, their gender and other significant sociological factors. We can also see that, from a social point of view, this is a two-way process, in the sense that, how a person behaves in relation to a trauma will not only be influenced by their social context, but will also, in turn, influence it. Consider, for example, the way in which the 9/11 atrocities have affected so much of the English-speaking world in general and the United States in particular.

- *Spiritual*. Third, there is also a spiritual dimension to trauma, as a traumatized person can feel that they are no longer sure of who they are and how they fit into the wider world. This can relate to religion, in so far as the reaction can be polarized. That is, people who are experiencing trauma can either lose their faith – feeling angry that, if there is a God, how can He allow such terrible things to happen – or the situation can go to the opposite extreme in which a person's faith is reaffirmed and strengthened. But even for people who have no religious background, spirituality is still an issue, in the sense that a trauma has the tendency to lead people to review their lives, to re-evaluate where they are now after such a devastating experience.

Trauma can be linked to both grief and crisis, but is also different from each of them. The similarities between trauma and grief are very strong. This is because we can see that, in effect, a person who has been traumatized has lost so much and is now undergoing a grief reaction in response to that loss. Such losses might include their sense of security, their sense of optimism or their feeling that all is well in the world and that they are safe. Trauma can shatter all of these and more, and so it is not surprising that we note significant grief reactions so often when we are dealing with people who have been traumatized in some way.

Trauma is also linked to crisis, in the sense that a trauma is also likely to be a crisis point. Trauma can result in a person feeling they are no longer able to cope, that they have to respond differently and so they find themselves in a crisis situation. These links are important because they help us to understand the complex interactions of trauma, grief and crisis. They are not just isolated aspects of human experience – they have much in common.

In terms of differences, trauma can be seen to be different from grief, in so far as the latter (as we shall see in Part II) is a process of healing and, although that may go awry at times, in the majority of cases there are successful outcomes to what has proven to be an extremely painful process. Trauma, by contrast, is something that will not necessarily lead to healing. There is a much higher likelihood that a person who has been traumatized will need professional help. Without this, there is the potential for the scar, as it were, of the psychosocial wound still to be felt years later. We shall return to this point below.

PRACTICE FOCUS 2.3

Mira was a single mother of two children, aged 5 and 7, who appeared to have no major difficulties in her life and was reasonably happy with her circumstances. However, all this was to change suddenly when, one night, there was a burglary in their home. She heard a noise downstairs and went to investigate. She found a young man in her living room. She started to scream but he grabbed her, covered her mouth and threatened her with a knife. He said he would rape her if she didn't stay quiet. He then demanded she show him where her purse was and, once he had that, he fled. Although Mira was not physically harmed in the incident, the psychological effect was clearly a traumatic one. She became very withdrawn, largely ignoring her children's needs and any other demands upon her. It was as if she had switched off from life or entered some sort of trance. Fortunately, her mother lived nearby and was able to ensure that the children were cared for, as Mira didn't even seem to be aware that they were in the room much of the time. She remained in this state for almost two months before she showed any sign of coming out of it. Her mother wondered whether she would ever totally recover from the experience.

Trauma is also different from crisis, in so far as a crisis involves a breakdown of homeostasis, while a trauma may involve this but does not have to. Some people can experience significant pain and even long-term harm as a result of the trauma, but they still manage to cope without the need for new ways of coping to emerge. In fact, this can often be part of the problem when it comes to trauma, in so far as the situation the person is in has now changed dramatically, but they may continue to cope in the same way as before, however ineffective that may be. They do not go through the potential healing of a grief process, nor do they encounter the potentially empowering experience of a crisis. It is as if they have become locked in to their problems as a result of the trauma. For example, someone who experiences a trauma may become withdrawn and depressed and thereby fail to address the issues presented by the trauma (see Practice focus 2.3).

Grief, crisis and trauma

To capture the similarities and differences across grief, crisis and trauma, it can be helpful to think in the following terms:

- *Grief* brings about significant changes that *challenge* our coping resources. As we grieve we feel the strain of having to cope with additional biological, psychological, social and spiritual pressures. Grief tends to instil a strong sense of vulnerability and insecurity and presents us with the task of developing new meanings that enable us to feel relatively safe and secure again. Where possible, professional helpers can try to help to make this a transformational experience – that is, one that entails growth and development.
- *Crisis* involves one or more changes that *overwhelm* our coping resources, leading to a situation in which we are forced into adopting new ways of coping in order to re-establish homeostasis. Crisis also tends to generate a strong sense of vulnerability and insecurity, and it is often this that motivates people in crisis to find new ways forward, to make changes that they

would perhaps not have entertained while in a state of homeostasis. Professional helpers can help to make sure that the person(s) in crisis, not only survive the crisis, but actually come out of it strengthened and empowered in some way (Thompson, 2011a).

- *Trauma* involves one or more sudden and drastic changes that *devastate* our coping resources, leaving us feeling totally at sea, at a loss as to how to go on. This tends to produce an extreme sense of vulnerability and insecurity, even to the point, in some trauma circumstances, of feeling that we are no longer sure who we are – the sense of insecurity is that intense. In some cases professional helpers can play a key role in helping traumatized individuals to achieve post-traumatic growth – that is, to emerge from the experience having grown in some way.

It is important to emphasize that trauma has significant implications in relation to grief. This can be seen to apply at two interconnected levels. First of all, a traumatized person is likely to be vulnerable to future losses and crises. That is, if a trauma experience has left somebody coping at a lower level, at a lower capacity for

Figure 2.1 Grief, crisis and trauma

dealing with life's challenges, then they are more likely to be plunged into crisis and to experience other losses as a result of their vulnerable position. For example, someone who has been traumatized as a result of being exposed to violence may then struggle to cope with any situation where violence becomes a possibility. This could then prevent that person from holding down a job if it means, for example, that they are no longer able to work with the general public.

Voice of experience 2.3

&&Sadly I have come across so many people who end up 'bumping along the bottom'. What I mean by that is people who have had some sort of major tragedy (or set of tragedies) in their life which has devastated them and, just as they are starting to climb out of the swamp they are in, another crisis or mishap drags them back down. Once you are in that swamp – in that hell – it doesn't take much to knock your fragile confidence and stop you from coping with what life is throwing at you.&&

Joanne, a mental health social worker

Second, trauma-related behaviour can lead to other losses or crises or even further trauma for others. A sad, but good, example of this can be seen to arise from what we now know about the way child abuse can traumatize some children and potentially have long-lasting detrimental effects throughout their lives (Tomlinson and Philpot, 2008). In particular, what we are aware of is that, while it certainly does not apply to all abused children, we know that some children who have been abused subsequently can go on to abuse other children (Rymaszewska and Philpot, 2006).

This, therefore, paints a complex picture in which trauma, grief and crisis interrelate in significant and potentially destructive ways. However, if we are well equipped with a good knowledge of how these three elements do interrelate with one another, then we are also in a stronger position to become involved in such scenarios in a constructive and empowering way. It could be argued that the greater the risk of harm as a result of grief, crisis and trauma, the better a position the professional helper is in to play a positive role in helping to ensure that, where possible, the outcomes of the situation are positive ones. This certainly 'ups the stakes' in terms of the contribution of professionals, which adds all the more weight to the idea that it is vitally important that we approach such matters with as strong a knowledge base as possible. To wrestle with the challenges of grief, crisis and trauma with little or no knowledge of what is involved in such complex scenarios can mean that the net result is that we make the problems worse, that we add to the pain and suffering rather than aid people in bearing them and that we miss what could be crucial opportunities to help people grow and develop as a result of the misfortunes that have befallen them.

A recurring theme in relation to grief, crisis and trauma is the way individuals can at times experience what could be called an emotional battering, that events conspire to produce a very strong negative emotional situation. This, then, can lead to people who are on the receiving end of such an emotional onslaught to feel and, in fact, be very vulnerable. This, in turn, can lead to further problems, partly because someone who is very vulnerable can subsequently be prone to further losses and crises, as I have already noted, but also partly because someone who is, in a sense, vulnerable as a result of an emotional battering may also become 'emotionally unavailable'. That is, they can withdraw their affection towards other people; they can isolate themselves, and thereby become alienated and subject to a whole range of other problems associated with social isolation as a result of this. The implications, then, of crisis and trauma for individuals, families, communities and society at large are therefore of quite significant proportions.

We should also not forget the spiritual dimensions of this subject matter. Someone who is in crisis or has been traumatized is likely to experience a degree of spiritual impoverishment, in the sense that they can lose their sense of direction, even lose their sense of who they are, temporarily at least. There can also be a loss of hope and, particularly if the result is withdrawal, there can be a reduction in 'connectedness'. There is a considerable irony here, in so far as it can be at the very time when people need their spiritual strength most and, in particular, when people need social support from other people, that their opportunity to be spiritually enriched and to benefit from connectedness can be at its lowest. This is a key point for professional helpers to bear in mind: in working with people who are in crisis, or who have been traumatized, their spiritual needs can be very significant.

Spirituality is closely linked to the idea of meaning making, and this is another theme that we can identify that applies to all three areas: grief, crisis and trauma. As we noted in Chapter 1, the process of grieving can be understood as a painful process of meaning reconstruction. Similarly, a crisis is often a crisis of meaning, in effect a spiritual crisis (Thompson, 2011a). As far as trauma is concerned, once again meaning can be seen to be a key factor, as Bracken (2003) explains, in describing traumatic experiences by using a chess analogy:

> there are times when the meaningfulness of the world is withdrawn – situations in which all the elements of our lives are still present but the background sense of coherence retreats. At these times it appears that the chequered board has been removed. The pieces remain in place but their connection to one another seems arbitrary. These are times when we are confronted with the sense that there is no ground at all beneath our feet and our lives come to lack direction and purpose. (p. 1)

Whenever we are dealing with issues relating to grief, crisis and trauma – individually or in combination – we therefore need to be tuned in to the central role of meaning. This will have implications for our discussions of professional practice later in the book.

Conclusion

This chapter has explored some very significant issues. Each of the two topics (crisis and trauma) could easily have provided enough issues to fill a chapter on their own and indeed, one or more books. They are both complex, multifaceted sets of issues. The way they interrelate with one another is also complex and demanding. The way the two of them then also interrelate with grief is also complex, so the picture that this chapter has painted is one in which grief, crisis and trauma interact and produce a very subtle and intricate set of dynamics that has significant implications, not only for people who are grieving, in crisis or traumatized, but also for helpers who are trying to support them through such difficult and demanding times.

We have seen, then, that while the medical profession uses the term trauma in a direct, literal sense to mean a wound to the body, in the helping professions more broadly, trauma refers to a psychosocial and spiritual experience. We therefore need to be able to understand and appreciate the psychological, sociological and spiritual dimensions of people's lives and, particularly, how those aspects relate to the situation they are currently wrestling with, as they go through a very difficult time. Without that knowledge and understanding, we can feel overwhelmed and at a loss as to what to do (see Chapter 5 for further discussion of these issues) and we can therefore be relatively ineffectual as helpers. It is to be hoped, then, that this chapter has established the importance of having a good understanding of crisis and trauma and how they relate to loss and grief.

POINTS TO PONDER

- In your area of work (or the area of work you are studying) what situations are you likely to encounter that could be crisis situations?
- In what ways might you encounter people who have been traumatized?
- Why is it important to understand that both crisis and trauma are closely linked to loss and grief?

Key texts

1. Everstine, D. S. and Everstine, L. (2006) *Strategic Interventions for People in Crisis, Trauma and Disaster*, Abingdon, Routledge.
2. Thompson, N. (2011) *Crisis Intervention,* 2nd edn, Lyme Regis, Russell House Publishing.
3. Wilson, J. P. (ed) (2006) *The Posttraumatic Self: Restoring Meaning and Wholeness to Personality*, London, Routledge.

3

The social context

Introduction

In this chapter I examine how grief has traditionally tended to be conceptualized primarily in (bio)psychological terms with relatively little attention being paid to the social context in which grief occurs and the sociological considerations that are applicable because of this. It shows how developing this wider perspective is important in terms of both theory and practice. It explores the significant role of cultural differences, as well as structural factors such as class, race, gender, age and so on. It draws on my earlier work in relation to discrimination and oppression and, in particular, the use of the PCS analysis framework (Thompson, 2011b; 2012). Some people may think it strange that I should be talking about discrimination and oppression when discussing grief, as the two sets of issues are rarely connected. However, this is just one example of how and why it is important to extend our understanding of grief beyond the traditional biopsychological approach.

Beyond the psychological

There has been a long-standing connection between grief and the notion of meaning. As long ago as 1974, Marris was writing about how grief has an impact on the way we make sense of things, in effect, on our meanings. More recently, writers such as Neimeyer (2001) and Attig (2011) have written extensively about the need to look at how meanings are changed by a grief experience. Indeed, this is the basis of meaning reconstruction theory (Neimeyer and

Anderson, 2002). It involves recognizing, as we saw in Chapter 1, that a major loss involves a significant loss of meaning, and that we can therefore understand the process of grieving as the painful, but necessary, process of developing new meanings, of reconstructing our world based on the changes that have been imposed upon us by the loss.

PRACTICE FOCUS 3.1

Jeannie had worked in the same office, with the same manager (Sheila) for almost eight years. She really enjoyed working there, particularly the strong sense of camaraderie that Sheila's skilled leadership had helped to generate. When Sheila died of a heart attack, Jeannie was devastated. She felt as though a huge hole had developed in her life and she wondered whether she would ever be able to fill it. She had not only lost an excellent boss and a good friend and colleague, she also felt that her working life had been turned upside down, that something that was so important as a basis of her happiness – and even her sense of who she was these days – had been taken from her. She now faced the long, painful and difficult task of rebuilding her life based on new understandings, new ways of living her life. She knew there was no going back, but she felt very uneasy about going forward, about what shape and meaning her new life would have without Sheila.

Many people would see this emphasis on meaning as primarily a psychological matter. However, it has to be recognized that the meanings we attach to the experiences we have are partly unique to us, but also partly a reflection of the cultural contexts in which we currently live and which would have shaped our upbringing. In this sense, meaning is both a psychological and a social phenomenon or, to put it more simply, it is *psychosocial*. Similarly, meaning is closely related to the concept of identity. Who we are is partly to do with the meanings that we have developed, the narrative of our life that we have written as it were, and so that, too, is social as well as psychological (Lawler, 2008). But also, identity is in large part formed by the social context in which we have developed that identity (Craib, 1998). That is, identity is largely social identity (Parekh, 2008).

Grief, then, is not purely a psychological phenomenon. It also has its roots in sociology. One particularly important example of this is the notion of disenfranchised grief which is associated with the work of Doka (1989, 2002). Disenfranchised grief refers to the type of grief which is not recognized or socially sanctioned in any way, thereby making it harder for the person grieving to deal with the challenges involved. This, according to Doka, can apply in three different ways:

1. The *relationship* can be disenfranchised. This refers to situations where there is something about the nature of the relationship that can mean that a loss is not recognized. This could apply to, for example, a gay couple who have not come out – that is, their relationship appears on the surface to be just two people of the same sex sharing a flat or house, but when one of the couple dies, it can then be extremely difficult for the surviving member of that couple to grieve as openly or intensely as they would like when, to all intents and purposes, they have lost a friend rather than a lover and life partner. This can have significant implications for the experience of grief and the extent to which social support is offered. It also has implications in terms of meaning for how the person who is in that situation can make sense of what has happened when their understanding could be very different from the understanding of significant people in their social network.
2. The *loss* is disenfranchised. This refers to the type of loss that cannot be socially recognized. A sad but significant example of this is suicide. Because of the stigma associated with suicide (Wertheimer, 2001), people who are grieving the loss of a loved one who has committed suicide can find that: (i) they do not get the full amount of social support that would otherwise have been on offer; and (ii) they struggle with the meaning-making element of grieving because of the complications brought about by the stigma associated with suicide. This stigma can apply at two levels: (i) it can be an objective type of stigma – that is, the stigma is in the eyes of other people

who look down on someone who has committed suicide; but (ii) it can also be subjective, in the sense that people grieving for someone who has committed suicide may themselves feel a sense of shame, that they may have internalized that stigma, with the result that they come to feel that the person concerned having taken their own life actually is a shameful thing. This can be linked in some circumstances to religious beliefs.

3 The *griever* may be disenfranchised. This refers to situations where particular groups of people can experience a major loss, but without having that loss recognized because of who they are – mainly because of stereotypical assumptions. For example, children may be disenfranchised in their grief because they may be excluded from, for example, funerals or other discussions around the loss of a key person in their life. People with learning disabilities can also be excluded because it is assumed that 'they' do not understand. This can cause major problems for people with learning disabilities who, because of their disability, may struggle to understand what is happening. The social exclusion that can accompany this can make it far worse. A third group who come into this category are older people. This is because it is often assumed that older people 'get used to loss' and therefore suffer very little when they experience a loss. In reality, the situation is likely to be the opposite, in the sense that grief can get harder to deal with in old age, rather than easier, because of the cumulative nature of loss. The idea that people somehow get used to loss is a very unhelpful and inaccurate one. My experience in working with older people over many years has convinced me that the idea that older people get used to loss is an ageist myth – cumulative loss was a far more common occurrence.

Voice of experience 3.1

❝We had a guest speaker at our team meeting once who talked to us about disenfranchised grief for people with learning disabilities. It was fascinating and really opened our eyes. It explained a lot about various

situations we had all encountered in our work and made us all determined
not to miss its significance in future. **"**
Kim, manager of a multidisciplinary learning disabilities team

These were the three elements of disenfranchised grief that were
associated with the ground-breaking work of Doka. However, we can
add two further classifications of disenfranchised grief. The first is
where losses occur in the workplace (Corr, 1998; Thompson,
2009a). It is not uncommon for workplaces to be operating on the
basis that a small number of days for compassionate leave is all that
is necessary before the individual can then resume work completely.
This reflects the fact that the significance of grief in the workplace
is often not fully appreciated. As Doka (1999) comments:

> One of the most common questions asked by survivors of a death
> is whether or not their responses are, in fact, normal. And often
> the response of others seems to invalidate their grief. Others may
> expect survivors to quickly let go of their grief and get on with
> their lives. The understanding that grief is a long, uneven process
> that affects individuals on a variety of levels – physical,
> emotional, cognitive, spiritual and behavioural – does not seem to
> be widely known. In fact, a study of clergy indicated that even
> these frontline professionals underestimated both the nature and
> duration of grief (Doka and Jendreski, 1985). (p. 5)

One further form of disenfranchisement arises when we consider
losses that are not directly death related. Indeed, these are often not
recognized as loss situations at all. We have well-established rituals
and social expectations in relation to bereavements, but where we
are talking about losses that can very often be just as significant, just
as devastating (but are not related to a death), these can be disenfranchised, in the sense that they are not recognized to anything like
the same extent as losses associated with bereavement. As we saw in
Chapter 1, such losses can be many and varied and can have a
significant impact, whether in isolation or in combination. If we look
carefully at disenfranchised grief, we can see that there can also be

significant issues arising because of the combination of disenfranchising factors. For example, we may have a person who is grieving in the workplace in relation to a loss that is not death related. If that person should also, for example, have a learning disability, then there would be further complications. It is therefore important to recognize that disenfranchised grief is not a static concept. It is one that is dynamic and involves the potential interactions of various aspects.

Disenfranchised grief is an important concept in its own right, but it is also highly significant as an example of the *social* context of grief because, while there are clearly significant psychological issues associated with disenfranchised grief, we have to recognize that its basis is in society in terms of social attitudes, stereotypes, social expectations and so on.

This is not to say that psychological issues are not relevant, but it is important to emphasize that the traditional narrow focus on psychological factors to the almost total exclusion of other concerns results in a distorted picture of the complexities of grief, and is therefore potentially dangerous. A distorted picture will prevent us from developing an understanding (theory) that does justice to the complexities of grief and can lead us in unhelpful directions in our efforts to help (practice).

The cultural context

We are, of course, all unique individuals, but we need to recognize that we are unique individuals within a social context (Pullen, Beech and Sims 2007; Thompson, 2012), and a key part of that social context or milieu is the cultural context. We grow up in at least one particular cultural setting and, as adults, are influenced by at least one set of cultural influences. Indeed, many people will be exposed to a wide variety of cultural influences as part of their upbringing and/or their later adult life experience. The net result is that everybody is part of at least one culture, and sometimes a wide range of cultural influences are being brought to bear on our understanding of the world. Culture is a significant influence on how we see ourselves, how we see the world and our place within it (and this therefore has important spiritual implications). It is not just a back-drop, not just an interesting set of different folkways, traditions or practices, but also a profound influence on how we perceive our social reality and, indeed, how we perceive ourselves within that reality.

PRACTICE FOCUS 3.2

Gaynor was a social worker in a childcare team in the north of England. She had fallen in love with Wales when she had gone there on holiday as a child, and so, when an opportunity to live and work in Wales came up, she grasped it very quickly and was delighted to be successful in her application. Before she went to work in Wales, she had not realized how many assumptions she had been making about the place and the people. To her, seeing bilingual signs and hearing Welsh spoken seemed just a slightly eccentric part of the local way of life. But, after living there for some time, she decided to learn to speak Welsh and to immerse herself in Welsh culture, with its myths and legends, arts, culture, music and politics. She could see just how significant issues of language and culture are and how they are signs of Wales having a very different cultural system from England. She realized now that, as a child, she had just seen Wales as England with a few quirks, but, after living in Wales, had come to accept how inaccurate and disrespectful that assumption was – and how it had prevented her from experiencing the cultural rich-ness she was now enjoying. (adapted from Thompson, 2010)

Culture can influence us in a variety of ways. It can shape how we think and how we perceive the world. For example, the concepts that we use in making sense of the world will be partly – largely, in fact – derived from our cultural understandings. For example, the western idea that we can ask a person how they are 'in themselves' is relatively meaningless to many people from eastern cultures who have no concept of 'in themselves'. This is because western cultures tend to have a very strongly individualistic focus, while so often eastern cultures have much more collective ways of seeing the world (Guirdham, 1999). So, even the way we think – the basic thinking tools or concepts that we use – owe much to our cultural context.

In addition to this, our emotional responses are generally circumscribed by our cultural background and current cultural location. For example, the fact that men and women often deal with emotional issues in different ways is not a matter of biology, but rather of cultural learning patterns (Fischer, 2000). This can be seen from the fact that different cultures express emotions in different ways and the way men and women respectively fit into those cultural patterns also differs from culture to culture or society to society. Of course, if it were simply a matter of biology, then such differences would not follow cultural patterns, but rather would be universal on the basis of our shared biology.

There are also significant behaviours that are culturally influenced. For example, we rely on rituals in a wide number of situations. These are particularly significant at times of change in our life (see the discussion of crisis and transition in Chapter 2). There can be rituals that help us to feel part of society, to feel that we have some sense of connectedness to other people, and so these again have spiritual implications, as well as psychological and sociological ones.

But, perhaps what is most important for present purposes is the recognition that cultural contexts shape the way we conceptualize loss and therefore the way we conceptualize grief reactions to that loss. There is now a significant literature base that gives us a wide variety of examples of these differences (see the 'Guide to further learning' at the end of the book). As Neimeyer (2006) comments:

> Although death, dying and bereavement are obviously universal phenomena, the meanings and practices with which people respond to them are intricately cultural and personal. This is perhaps most obviously true with respect to the immense diversity of secular and spiritual frameworks with which human communities conceptualize the state of death, but it is no less true of the variety of ways in which people engage the dying process and the ways survivors grieve in death's aftermath. (p. ix)

Voice of experience 3.2

❝My first ward experience was in a hospital in a rural area very similar to where I grew up. It was very traditional. My second ward experience, though, was very, very different. It was in a hospital covering a very multicultural inner-city area. To begin with I just couldn't get over how varied the people I nursed were; they were from so many different backgrounds – I suppose we would call it diversity these days. It was a bit scary at first 'cause I felt out of my depth, but once I got used to it, I really enjoyed learning about the people I was working with and their different cultural backgrounds. It was fascinating, and so different from my very sheltered upbringing in a more or less all-white small town.❞

Caroline, a paediatric nurse

As I have already noted, a key part of culture is a set of rituals. These are, in a sense, a set of established ways of behaving in circumstances that are defined (within that particular culture) as significant, not only for the individuals concerned, but for the community as a whole within that culture. Rituals have a strong function in terms of social bonding, and help to create a sense of security (particularly ontological security which is concerned with our sense of how we fit into the world). There are two types of ritual: one is in relation to transition. This refers to rituals that acknowledge a significant change and therefore help people to come together to acknowledge that change and to help each other through it. A funeral is a good example of a ritual of transition. It enables people to formally acknowledge the loss that has occurred, the change that has taken place, and it provides a social space in which people can express emotion and connect with one another in doing so. It therefore has a very important cultural role in helping us to deal with situations of loss.

A further example of a ritual of transition would be the situation where, after a change (it may be a loss, but does not have to be), a person may then remove all vestiges that may remind them of the previous situation. For example, somebody who separates from a partner through divorce may subsequently remove all photographs or other items that are reminiscent of the earlier relationship. It is as if it were a form of ritual cleansing. That, too, is a ritual of transition – it marks a significant change.

The other type of ritual is a ritual of continuity. This is the type of cultural process or event that emphasizes continuity. While a change may have taken place, there still remains a strong degree of continuity. In relation to loss and grief, a good example of this would be a memorial service. While a funeral emphasizes the change that has occurred, a memorial service – by focusing on celebrating the life of the person who has died – is emphasizing how they, through the ongoing influence of their work, for example, will continue to have a presence, will continue to shape or influence what happens. It is interesting to note that, in some cultures, this distinction between a funeral and a memorial service is blurred. For example, the Irish tradition of holding a wake is more in keeping with a ritual of continuity, where the emphasis is on celebrating the life of the person who has passed away, rather than (or as well as) acknowledging the loss and the sadness associated with it. This again emphasizes the significance of cultural diversity, how different cultures will be called upon to deal with the same life challenges, but will do so in different ways, in ways that reflect the characteristics of that culture.

This emphasis on the cultural context takes us another step away from the narrow focus on psychological factors. It helps us to understand that, when we are looking at loss and grief issues, we do have to take account of the psychological factors, but also have to relate them at the very least to the cultural context. I would also argue that it is important to consider the structural context, and it is to this that we now turn.

The structural context

What is meant by structure is the idea that society is not a level playing field, that we can see how people are structured into different groups in line with what sociologists call 'social divisions' (Payne, 2006). That is, acknowledging the structural context involves recognizing that people do not function in isolation, and do not exist within only a cultural context, but also within a context of hierarchical relationships, shaped by such key factors as:

- *Class.* This refers to our socioeconomic position: whether we are at the bottom of the wealth league or at the top of it or, as in the case of most of us, somewhere in between. All these issues will be significant in terms of our identity, and will therefore be significant in shaping how we respond to loss situations (Bevan, 2002).

- *Race.* This is a contentious issue at one level because the idea that there are distinct biological races is one that cannot be supported (Malik, 1996, 2008). However, it would be naive not to recognize that so many societies operate on the basis of assumed racial divisions, and we therefore have to take racism quite seriously as a social problem (Back and Solomos, 2009; Thompson, 2011b). This is rarely connected with matters to do with loss and grief, but if we look more closely at the connection between grief and race, we begin to realize that there are in fact some very significant links, and the fact that they tend to be neglected and not given the attention they deserve adds to a further sense of disenfranchisement. Desai and Bevan (2002) make apt comment when they argue that:

  > The collective and individual sense of bereft isolation and loss of expression arising from their spiritual needs being disenfranchised will compound the dying experience of those already disadvantaged through race. (p. 75)

  See also Barrett (1998) and Rosenblatt and Wallace (2005).

- *Gender.* For a very long time, it was assumed that people grieve in the same way, whether men or women. We now have a growing body of research that demonstrates that this was a mistaken assumption. In particular, the work of Doka and Martin (2010) has shown that there are significant differences between the genders in terms of how grief issues are conceptualized and responded to.

- *Age.* As we move through the life course, issues to do with grief can change significantly. For example, children will understand grief differently according to their level of development (Walter and McCoyd, 2009) and, later on in the life course, where we are in this process – this trajectory from birth to death – will also shape how we understand grief (Thompson and Thompson, 2004; S. Thompson, 2007). We therefore have to take account of age as a key social factor in terms of grief.

- *Disability*. Whether or not somebody is disabled is partly a *physical* matter to do with impairment, but is also largely a *social* matter, in terms of how society *dis*ables certain people through attitudes towards them, through social practices and institutions that exclude them in some way (Oliver, 2004; Oliver and Sapey, 2005). It would be naive, then, to assume that such significant social factors have no bearing on the experience of grief for disabled people (see Sapey, 2002, for an interesting discussion of such issues).

- *Sexuality*. Whether a person's sexual identity is gay, straight, bisexual or transgender is partly a personal matter, but also relates to the wider social and structural context. If we consider these issues carefully we can begin to recognize that there are significant implications here in terms of loss and grief (not least in relation to disenfranchised grief as discussed above). If we consider losses that are not death related, we can identify a number of ways in which 'heterosexism' (discrimination on the grounds of sexuality – Carabine, 2004) can produce a range of losses that are rooted in the stigma, marginalization and disempowerment associated with such discrimination (Thompson and Colón, 2004).

- *Language*. The language one speaks is not only an important identity marker (and therefore an important aspect of the social structure), it is also very significant in terms of how we deal with grief. For example, if someone speaks a minority language within the society they currently live in, the non-availability of bereavement counselling in their first language may place them at a significant disadvantage in terms of the support available to them.

PRACTICE FOCUS 3.3

Darren had recently completed his training as a counsellor and was now working on an unpaid basis with a voluntary organization in order to get the experience he needed to become accredited with his professional body. The voluntary organization had various schemes and programmes, including one that involved providing support and advocacy services for gay people. This was a new field to Darren and he was keen to learn as much as he could so that he could be helpful to his clients. One of the first things to strike him was how much loss the people he was working with seemed to have experienced. As time went on he got to understand more and more about how this situation had come about. In particular, he started to see how so many of the loss experiences were related to discrimination. This really hit home to him when he worked with Barry, a young man who had received so much hostility when his work colleagues found out that he was gay that he had to give his job up. He then felt a failure and also felt powerless to do anything about the situation. This, Darren could see, involved a wide range of losses for Barry. Darren could also see that this was not an isolated, atypical case.

These seven social divisions are not the only ones, but space does not permit a fuller analysis of the full range of potential ways in which social structure can play a key role in shaping a person's experience of loss and grief. We should also recognize that, for ease of exposition, I have discussed each of these divisions in isolation, one at a time. The reality, however, for actual living people is that these are interconnected dimensions of their experience, rather than isolated phenomena, and so we have to understand the potential for combined effects (Thompson, 2011b). For example, a black elderly woman may face issues that relate to class, race, gender and age and possibly also disability, sexuality and language. It is important, then, that we do not see this simple classification as being a reflection of the actual complexities of lived experience. They can help us, however, to understand that it is important not to lose sight of how the structural context of people's lives is a key part of their experience of loss, and, once again, to recognize that grief is not purely a psychological phenomenon.

Grief in social context

Howarth (2007) puts forward a telling argument when she states that:

> The concept of social diversity is broad-ranging and not solely confined to ethnic differences. All social distinctions, such as social class, ethnicity, gender, age sexuality and disability, help to give shape and meaning to experiences of dying, death and grief. Indeed, the recognition of difference should be central to any theoretical understanding of the nature of death in society. (p. 38)

While I would very much want to support this argument (as my comments throughout this chapter confirm), I would also want to extend it, to argue that an understanding of difference (and the personal, cultural and structural factors associated with it – Thompson, 2011b) should be central to any theoretical understanding of not only death, but also of any experience of loss and grief in society.

Given how painful, powerful, disruptive, disorienting and intense grief experiences are, and how intimately they affect us, it is not at all surprising that we tend to focus on the *personal* dimensions of loss and grief. This is reflected in both theory and practice.

Theory

The literature base relating to death, dying and bereavement and to loss and grief more broadly tends to adopt a predominantly psychological focus which is strongly individualistic in its emphasis. This is not to say that there is no strong body of sociological literature – as that is certainly not the case: see Auger (2000); Howarth (2007); and Kellehear (2007), for example – but in the overall scheme of things in relation to our foundations of knowledge, the social context literature is clearly peripheral to the psychological core.

Practice

A close examination of the literature relating to the helping professions will soon reveal a picture of practice which is fundamentally individualistic in its focus (or 'atomistic', to use the technical term). While it is good to see that individual, psychological matters are receiving a great deal of attention, it is potentially very problematic for these to feature at the expense of the equally important sociological aspects of the situation (and, indeed, the spiritual ones too – Moss, 2002). At its worst, individualization can manifest itself as a medicalized approach to grief, as if what is needed is treatment for an illness (Furedi, 2004; Kellehear, 2005), as discussed in the Introduction. Without a sociological dimension to our understanding we may:

- Disrespect someone's culture and thereby behave towards them in ways that are counterproductive when it comes to trying to be helpful. This is important at any time, but is particularly significant when we are trying to support someone who is grieving and therefore likely to be feeling vulnerable and insecure.
- Make misleading and discriminatory sexist assumptions about how people (should) grieve, by failing to recognize the significance of gendered patterns of grieving (Riches, 2002).
- Reinforce the problems associated with disenfranchised grief.
- Inhibit people from grieving in ways which are best suited to them by adopting a medicalized approach to loss and grief which makes little or no allowance for social diversity.

Voice of experience 3.3

❛❛I used to work with a consultant who seemed to regard grief as an illness and would ask about what 'treatment' we could offer to patients who had suffered a bereavement. We would come up with a programme of help whenever we needed to, but most of the time people just needed understanding and reassurance, but certainly not 'treatment'.❜❜

Kara, an occupational therapist working with older people

Conclusion

A key theme of this book is the idea that grief is something that needs to be understood *holistically* – that is, not simply as a psychological matter, but as a bio-psychosocial and spiritual phenomenon. This chapter has emphasized the social aspects of that combination of influences, while arguing that these need to inform our understanding *alongside* the psychological and spiritual elements and not instead of them. It is also important to note that an emphasis on the social elements moves us away from the tendency to medicalize situations of grief and therefore to focus too closely or too narrowly on the biological aspects of a grieving person's life. To see someone who is grieving simply as an 'organism', rather than as a person, is clearly a mistake, and it is to be hoped that this chapter has helped to emphasize the need for this more holistic perspective.

What we need to recognize, then, is that it does not matter how personal, private or intimate a grief experience may be, it none the less happens in a social context, and that social context includes both cultural and structural dimensions. If we ignore or neglect the significance of that social context, we risk distorting a very complex situation and thereby potentially making the situation worse.

POINTS TO PONDER

- In what ways has your own cultural background influenced the way you understand and experience loss and grief?
- How might structural inequalities affect how people grieve?
- Why is it important to adopt a holistic perspective?

Key texts

1. Howarth, G. (2007) *Death & Dying: A Sociological Introduction*, Cambridge, Polity Press.
2. Rosenblatt, P. C. and Wallace, B. R. (2005) *African American Grief*, Hove, Routledge.
3. Doka, K. J. and Martin, T. L. (2010) *Grieving Beyond Gender: Understanding the Ways Men and Women Mourn*, New York, Routledge.

Part II

Grief and healing

Introduction

As we noted earlier, one very common misunderstanding is the idea that if someone is grieving, then they necessarily need help. Very many people cope with a major loss without any help at all. Sometimes – very often in fact – the only help that is needed is the informal support of family, friends and so on. It is only in a minority of cases that people need professional help. These are the sorts of situations we will focus on more in Part III. In Part II, by contrast, the focus is on how grief can be seen as a process of healing. It is a constructive process of what we might call 'spiritual healing', so it is not a medical matter (and it is certainly a mistake to see grief as a *mental* illness). Grief can bring problems, but it is not necessarily a problem in itself, or at least not the sort of problem that will necessarily need professional intervention. In some respects, grief can be seen as a solution as well as a problem. It is a means of coping with a very difficult situation and can therefore be seen as a positive, if painful, process. It is for this reason that Schneider (2000) is adamant, and quite rightly so, that we should be very careful not to confuse grief and depression.

Part II is divided into three chapters, the first of which, 'Experiencing Grief', looks at grief from the point of view of the person who is grieving. It considers the different reactions to grief that are experienced and considers the implications of this for the person concerned.

Chapter 5 takes a parallel view, but looks at grief from the point of view of the person who is offering help and provides some important insights in relation to how we can respond to grief effectively. This is followed by Chapter 6 in which the professional response is our major focus. This builds on the work of Chapter 5, but focuses more specifically on the factors that a professional helper needs to take into account if they are to be an effective helper in supporting somebody through a difficult and perhaps problematic grief experience.

4

Experiencing grief

Introduction

Chapter 4 is concerned with how people react to a major loss, with the behavioural, cognitive, emotional, physical and spiritual changes that are characteristic of grief. Its aim is to help you to develop empathy by enabling you to become more in tune with the intense reactions that grieving people are likely to experience. The chapter incorporates both theoretical and practical aspects of this central feature of this important subject matter. It also shows how the diversity of reactions can make a key difference to our understanding of the complexities involved. It again challenges the common assumption that grieving is something that follows a standard pattern.

In an earlier work (Thompson, 2009b) I talked about the think-feel-do framework which emphasizes that, if we are to understand what makes people tick, we need to think in terms of thoughts, feelings and actions or, to use the technical terms: cognitive, affective and behavioural factors. To this we need to add the significance of body and spirit. When we combine these elements, we start to get a *holistic* picture, an overview that gives us what many people would call 'the big picture', rather than focusing narrowly on one or maybe two aspects of what in reality is a very complex and broad whole (see Figure 4.1).

In this chapter, then, I am going to look at five different sets of factors: cognitive, emotional, behavioural, physical and spiritual. Let us begin by looking at how grief affects how we think.

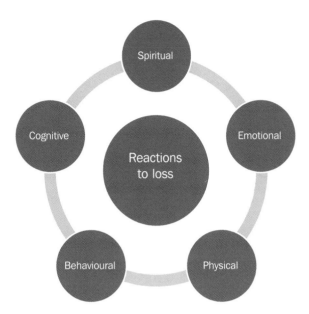

Figure 4.1 Reactions to loss

Cognitive reactions

Cognitive refers to thinking processes and memory and both of these can be significantly impaired by grief. When somebody is in the throes of grief, they can find it difficult to remember, difficult to think clearly or to concentrate, and also their thinking time may be affected – that is, they may experience slowness of reaction. This can have significant implications in terms of such things as driving a car or operating potentially dangerous machinery. It is therefore important to be aware of this aspect of grief, as it is important to avoid accidents at any time, but particularly at times when people have enough to contend with because of their current experiences of grief.

The example in Practice focus 4.1 is perhaps an extreme one, but less extreme examples are very common, and so we need to be tuned in to the potential for harm that exist in such situations.

> PRACTICE FOCUS 4.1
>
> Paul was the deputy manager of a children's home. He was driving to
> work one day when a lorry came straight across a roundabout and
> crashed into the side of his car. Fortunately, the lorry struck the car
> behind where Paul was sitting so, while the car was damaged beyond
> repair and he was severely shaken and shocked by the incident, he
> escaped unhurt. Later that day the police officer who attended the scene
> visited Paul at home to take a statement from him, as the police were
> considering prosecuting the driver for dangerous driving. The police offi-
> cer explained to Paul that he had interviewed the lorry driver and, when
> he asked him why he had not stopped at the roundabout, he replied that
> he had not even noticed the roundabout there. He went on to explain to
> the officer that his wife had left him the previous day and he was, in
> effect, driving around in a daze. His grief had rendered him incapable of
> concentrating on the task of driving safely.

However, this is not the only way in which grief can produce a
cognitive reaction. Depression is also associated with grief
(although it is important not to confuse depression and grief which
superficially can look very similar – see Schneider, 2000).
Depression is partly an emotional matter, but it is also something
that can have a profound effect on our thinking. Our perspective on
the world can be very significantly affected by grief, resulting in a
degree of pessimism and a tendency to think in predominantly negative terms.

Grief can also affect our thinking patterns in terms of leading us
to assume that we are going mad. Again it is important that we
understand this – partly because, from a theoretical point of view,
we will have an incomplete and distorted understanding of grief if
we are unaware of the significance of this issue, and partly from a
practical point of view, we will miss the opportunity to help people
(by reassuring them that they are not 'going mad' and that such
thoughts are perfectly normal and unproblematic). When grief is
already bringing a significant amount of extra pressure to our lives,
anxieties about possibly going mad are an unwelcome set of further
(unnecessary) pressures.

So, why might some grieving people fear that they are losing their sanity? Basically, it is because the intensity of the situation can lead to what superficially seem bizarre assumptions, bizarre thoughts and patterns of making sense of situations. Consider the following three examples:

1. *Laying the table.* I have encountered the situation many times where, for example, someone's spouse dies, but for weeks, months or even years after the loss, when preparing a meal they continue to lay the table for two people and not just for one. From the outside, this may seem to be a reflection of insane behaviour, but it is important to recognize that this is perfectly normal, and it is just one coping mechanism among many. If we cast our minds back to the discussion of rituals of continuity in Chapter 3, we can see that, in that context, this sort of behaviour, and the thinking behind it, make perfect sense.

2. *Spotting the deceased in a crowd.* This is another very common reaction which superficially seems to be a reflection of mental health problems, but, in reality, is nothing of the sort. Because we may be thinking a lot about somebody who mattered to us who is now no longer with us, then it is very easy to see somebody in a crowd who in some way reminds us of that person, and for our initial reaction to be that of assuming that it is that person, even though we know full well that it cannot be possible. Similarly, it is possible for people to go to a particular place that they associated with a person who has died and to expect to see that person there, until it suddenly dawns on them that this is not possible, and they then feel very foolish and perhaps again wonder: am I going mad? Once again, this is perfectly normal behaviour and nothing to worry about. It is not a sign of any sort of mental health problem.

3. *'It doesn't seem real'.* Sometimes it takes a while for our heart to catch up, with our head. That is, we may know that a significant loss has occurred, our thinking processes have clearly registered the fact, but it still does not seem real; it still does not feel as though it has actually happened. This sort of shock

reaction is again perfectly common and nothing to worry about.

Voice of experience 4.1

❝A very common feature of my job is reassuring people that they are not going mad. I give them examples of some of the weird and wonderful things I have come across over the years that people have done when grieving – all of them perfectly normal and nothing to worry about. That little bit of reassurance can go a long way.❞

Siân, a counsellor

While it is very easy for me to state in the abstract that these things are nothing to worry about, this does not alter the fact that, for people who are going through this sort of process or a combination of these factors, they can still feel very worried about what is happening. If we, in our efforts to help people who are grieving, encounter such situations, it is therefore important that we give them appropriate reassurance that they are not going mad and that these issues are very strongly associated with a grief reaction (and that we have known about these for a long time). In this way, we can offer a degree of realistic reassurance that can help people to appreciate that what is happening to them is not a process of losing their sanity, but rather a process of developing new meanings as a result of the loss or losses they have experienced – as Attig (2001) aptly puts it, they are 'relearning the world'.

Overall, then, there are many ways in which our thinking processes, our concentration and our memory can be affected by grief. Some of them can be quite worrying – for example, lack of concentration or slowness of reaction may make us (temporarily) unsafe as drivers – see Practice focus 4.1. However, others may superficially seem to be worrying, but in reality do not need to be the basis of any real concern.

Emotional reactions

There can be a wide range of emotional reactions to a loss. Emotions can include sadness, bitterness, resentment, disappointment, anxiety, confusion, a lack of confidence, anger, a sense of guilt (I will return to this point below) and even relief. This last example is particularly important, because a feeling of guilt, even where there is nothing to actually be guilty about, can lead to a sense of being on a roller-coaster, with the effect that, just as somebody is starting to feel stronger, to feel the loss less acutely, a sense of guilt can then plunge them back into what could possibly be the depths of despair. This reflects the dual process theory we discussed in Chapter 1 (Stroebe and Schut, 1999) where people will oscillate between loss orientation (looking back over who or what has been lost) and restoration orientation (looking forward, to rebuild our lives).

What is strongly characteristic of our emotional reactions at a time of grief is a very powerful sense of insecurity and vulnerability. This is often described as 'ontological insecurity'. This technical term refers to the type of insecurity that is not a specific insecurity (for example, worrying about being burgled), but rather a wider sense of existential insecurity, an overall feeling of vulnerability that can have important psychological, social and spiritual consequences. We should recognize that ontological insecurity is an important concept because, at times of significant grief, this form of insecurity can have a profound effect on us, leaving us feeling very vulnerable and very unconfident in terms of how to go about dealing with the challenges we face, both the specific challenges of coping with our loss(es) and the general challenges of getting on with our life.

One important distinction to make in terms of the emotional response to grief is that between emotion that is directed inwardly and emotion that is directed outwardly. Where the emotion goes in an inwards direction, it can result in withdrawal, or even depression, and can sometimes be experienced as a sense of guilt. Consider, for example, where a person feels angry and bitter about a loss, but does not express this in an outward direction. They internalize it, they hold it within, as it were. This can then produce a feeling that is very close to a sense of guilt, even though objectively they may have nothing to feel guilty about. Where such anger or bitterness is expressed outwardly, it can manifest itself as anger towards others, or even aggression and violence. In many circumstances, people who are grieving and feel angry about their loss can be looking for somebody to blame. This is a way of dealing with the intense anger they experience. For example, when somebody has experienced a loss as a result of crime, then there can be a very strong intense emotional reaction towards the perpetrator of the crime – for example, wanting them to receive a very severe punishment, perhaps the severest punishment available within the legal system, or even going so far as to campaign for more severe penalties.

It is important to recognize emotions as existential phenomena. We should see them as psychosocial and, indeed, spiritual. So, while it is important to recognize that there is a biological basis to

---

PRACTICE FOCUS 4.2

Mark was a volunteer in a Citizens' Advice Bureau. He had been involved for just over two months and was doing very well when Mrs Hargreaves came in to see him. Her husband had died, leaving her very unsure of what she needed to do in terms of banking arrangements, pensions and related matters, as her late husband had dealt with such matters over the years. Mark did his usual thorough job of looking up the information she needed and guiding her in the right direction. He also did it in a very polite and friendly manner as he usually did. Mrs Hargreaves thanked him for his help and left to start the process of sorting out the matters he had advised her about. On the surface it seemed as though Mark had done a very good job. However, he couldn't help feeling dissatisfied. For days afterwards he kept mulling it over in his mind and wondering what he could have done differently. Eventually it got to him so much that he sought the advice of a very experienced colleague. After this discussion Mark could fully understand why he had felt uneasy about his discussion. He was helped to understand that he had helped Mrs Hargreaves in a very logical, rational way, giving her the information and advice she needed, but he had not really taken account of the feelings involved – hers and his own. He had tried to deal with it as if it were a perfectly normal interaction, when in reality it was far from that – and that was what had left him feeling so uncomfortable. He realized that he had some learning to do about the emotional side of working with people – especially people deep in grief.

---

emotions, they are not purely biological matters. Emotions have important psychological causes and consequences – for example, in relation to factors to do with meaning making, as discussed in Chapter 3. There are also social aspects in terms of how society expects people to express emotion and whether that expression of emotion is encouraged or at least accepted, or whether it is discouraged or even, in some cases, punished or penalized (Barbalet, 2002). Emotions are also spiritual, in the sense that they relate to our sense of who we are and how we fit into the wider world. A significant loss experience can have such a profound emotional impact on us that we can, temporarily at least, lose sight of our spiritual bearings (Nicholls, 2007).

Clearly, then, it is not just the cognitive reactions to a loss that are important, but also the emotional ones. The two sets of factors will also, of course, interact and influence each other.

Behavioural reactions

In many ways, the way a person reacts in terms of their behaviour will be as a consequence of their cognitive and emotional responses. That is, how we behave will owe much to how we think and how we feel (hence the think-feel-do framework I referred to earlier).

A person's behaviour in a grief situation can be extreme at times. For example, there can be extreme activity where he or she is very busy, as if they are trying to fill the emptiness that the loss has brought to their lives. But, behaviour can also go to the opposite extreme – that of inactivity, and so a person who is grieving may have no energy, no impetus to go about their daily tasks, and this can create significant problems that can add to the difficulties of their grieving.

Behaviour can also be extreme in terms of being extremely constructive or extremely destructive. An example of the former would be someone who has experienced a major loss trying to do things in ways which reflect the importance of their loss. In this way, somebody who has lost a loved one through cancer, for example, may become a volunteer at their local hospice, and become a very energetic and valued contributor to the important work of that hospice. At the other extreme, a person's behaviour as a result of grief can be very destructive; the pain and suffering they experience can drive them to inflicting pain and suffering on other people. This is an important consideration in terms of how grief can contribute to social problems, and so this is a point to which we will return in Chapter 9. It is also a significant consideration in relation to 'complicated' grieving, as the reaction to such destructive behaviour can cause additional difficulties for the grieving person (for example, losing their job or losing the support of one or more important people). This issue is therefore relevant to the issues we will be discussing in Chapter 7.

Another notable aspect of behaviour is what is known as 'searching'. As a result of the sense of emptiness associated with a major loss, the grieving person may then adopt a pattern of searching. They have this strong feeling that there is something missing and they try to find it. Sometimes that can be done in quite an extreme way. In this way, a grieving person can be trying all sorts of new activities, new hobbies and interests, perhaps exploring different types of work, as if there were an answer to be found somewhere. This is not necessarily a problem, and a small degree of searching is something that is quite common and not necessarily destructive or problematic. However, when taken to extremes, it can lead to problems for that individual and his or her family or colleagues.

Linking back to the earlier comments I made about how, from an emotional point of view, a grieving person may become quite angry, when it comes to exploring the behavioural dimension, we can see that this may go a step further. It can reach the point where what the grieving person seems to be doing is trying to pick a fight, either with a specific individual or with anyone who just happens to get in the way. So, for example, where they are in disagreement with somebody, instead of trying to deal with that disagreement through normal channels, normal, civilized ways of dealing with such issues, they may become aggressive and antagonistic towards the other person. They may develop a habit of doing this and therefore find themselves in difficulties. It is therefore very important, in working with a person who is grieving who adopts this coping method, that we do not allow them to pick a fight with us, that we are suitably tactful and restrained to deal with what can be a significant amount of provocation at times. We need to remember that this is a by-product, as it were, of their grief and help them through it, rather than make the situation worse by allowing our own feelings to dominate the situation – for example, by responding to their aggression with our own indignation or, worse still, our own aggression.

Voice of experience 4.2

❝I have worked with young people in care for almost ten years now and one thing I have realized is that they tend to have a lot of loss experiences before they come to us and, if we are not careful, end up having more loss experiences while they are with us. One result of this is that we often come across behaviour that is quite provocative. Just labelling it as 'challenging behaviour' and trying to stamp it out is no way to deal with it, although I know some people do. We need to see it in context if we are really going to be able to help.**❞**

Nasreen, a residential child care worker

And finally, in terms of behaviour, a well-established behavioural pattern is that of mimicking the deceased. This is generally not deliberate; it is something that emerges without the grieving person realizing what is happening. In such circumstances they may adopt, for example, the mannerisms of the person they have lost. This is probably because they are thinking (and feeling) a great deal about the person they have lost, and therefore find themselves unwittingly reproducing their behaviour in various ways.

Overall, then, the behavioural dimension forms another set of important factors to be aware of in trying to understand how a grieving person may be reacting. These behavioural issues, as I noted above, are closely linked to the cognitive and emotional reactions but these three aspects of the psychological domain (cognitive, affective and behavioural) are not the only ones. We also need to consider what I referred to earlier as body and soul. So let us now move on to look at, to begin with, physical reactions and then later, spiritual ones.

Physical reactions

In effect, when a person is grieving, they are experiencing a stress reaction. That is, what is happening in their body is what happens when people are stressed generally: their body is reacting in the ways it would do if it were under a strain for other reasons. This can result in a variety of different physical responses. The main ones are as follows:

- *Exacerbation of pre-existing conditions.* This means that, where somebody already has a medical condition, the strain associated with grief can make it worse. For example, if somebody has a heart condition, then they can be at greater risk of a heart attack as a result of the stress associated with grief. At a less extreme level, it can apply to other conditions that are not necessarily life threatening, For example, someone with very mild asthma may find that, when they are grieving, their asthma is worse, without necessarily reaching a level where it is critical.
- *Stress-related conditions.* This refers to the development of new medical conditions brought about by the stress associated with the grief reaction. A very common one is ulcerative colitis. This refers to an inflammation of the colon (part of the bowel system) which becomes ulcerated, leading to considerable pain and discomfort. Less severely, there can be headaches, stomach upsets and general feelings of debility as a result of the physical strain brought about by the psychosocial and spiritual experience of a significant loss.
- *Appetite.* This can apply in one of two ways. At one extreme, what can be very common is for people to lose their appetite altogether – that is, to find it very difficult to face food, and they may need a lot of encouragement to make sure that they do not make themselves ill by neglecting their dietary requirements. At the other extreme, what can happen is that the grieving person can indulge in comfort eating. They find themselves eating far more than they normally would do and, in

particular, eating the sorts of foods that, because of their high sugar or fat levels, offer a degree of psychological comfort, but also have significant negative implications for health.

- *Sleep.* This can also be applicable in two directions. People can find it very difficult to sleep because they keep mulling over in their mind issues to do with who or what they have lost (this is often referred to as 'rumination'). They find it very difficult to get to sleep or they may wake up very early and not be able to get back to sleep because, once their mind becomes active again, they find it difficult to switch off and go back to sleep. It can also apply at the other extreme, in the sense that a person who is grieving may become quite inactive and lethargic and may therefore sleep more than usual.

- *Fitness.* Levels of exercise can also be reduced. This is particularly significant, as it can relate to the other potentially problematic physical aspects of grief. So, if somebody who normally exercises to a reasonable level then ceases to do so, because they feel so overwhelmed by their sense of loss, this can then have an impact on their appetite, their sleep patterns and so on. Ironically, then, at a time when exercise could do them the most good, this could well be the time when they are least likely to actively engage in exercise.

These four sets of issues then add to the earlier three to show how we again need a good understanding of the impact grief can have on people's lives if we are to be sufficiently well equipped to help them through their difficulties.

Spiritual reactions

I mentioned earlier that one emotional response to grieving is a strong sense of emptiness. There can also be a lack of meaning, a sense that life no longer makes sense and, linked to this, there can be a strong undermining of identity. All these add up to what could be called 'spiritual impoverishment'. Added to this can be a strong sense of hopelessness, producing a situation which also has spiritual

---

PRACTICE FOCUS 4.3

Eirwen was the deputy manager of a care home for older people. She was a trained and experienced nurse and was very keen to help residents stay healthy for as long as they could. She therefore took a keen interest in diet and nutrition issues and promoted exercise wherever she could. For the most part she was pleased with the positive results she achieved as a consequence of her efforts, but she always wanted to do even better. She got the chance to do this when she attended a training course about helping older people cope with grief. As part of the course the participants discussed the various effects and manifestations of grieving, Eirwen was particularly interested in the physical aspects. The course helped her to realize that this was an aspect of health promotion that she had not considered. She therefore went away from the course with a lot of food for thought about how she could incorporate her new learning into her work.

---

implications. Somebody who has experienced one or more significant losses, for example, may find it difficult to sustain any sense of hope, and so that too can add to a sense of spiritual loss, as well as an objective loss of the person or thing that mattered to us.

Voice of experience 4.3

❝From time to time I get the opportunity to teach health professionals at the local university. I try to get across the point that, while my own personal sense of spirituality is deeply rooted in the Christian church, everyone has spiritual needs, whether they are religious or not. We all need to be helped to find purpose, direction, meaning and hope at times in our lives, especially times of loss.**❞**

Colin, a hospital chaplain

However, we also have to recognize that this spiritual reaction can be a positive one. We will discuss later the significance of transformational grief, and so it is important to note here that a major loss can result in a spiritual transformation, a sense of spiritual renewal. This may take a religious form for many people, but can also take a non-religious form for others. As Holloway (2005) puts it: 'there is a rich and diverse range of human spiritualities in the world, and countless people follow them without reference to religion or any necessary sense of God' (p. xi). A renewed sense of who we are and how we fit into the wider scheme of things can be one positive effect of a loss, part of the silver lining.

Moss, an important commentator on spirituality in the helping professions, draws important links between spirituality and the ability to offer genuine help to people who are grieving:

> Those of us who seek to offer help, support and care to others in their moments of pain will ourselves from time to time have our own pain and emotional scar tissue to deal with. This, too, is what spirituality must be about, so that our hurts and wounds do not get in the way of our reaching out to others. Perhaps we are all wounded; perhaps the skill of being able to help others is to learn the art of becoming 'wounded healers,' in Nouen's (1966) phrase, or at least to be 'wounded helpers.' Maybe it is our spirituality that enables us so to tune, or at times to re-tune, our humanity that we can learn that creative, vulnerable openness which enables our pain to sensitize us to the pain of others, and not to flinch from it. (2007a, pp. 86–7)

Specifically in relation to religion, it is important to reiterate the point I made earlier that, at such intense times, some people may find it difficult to hold on to their religious faith while others will have that faith reaffirmed. As Doka (1999) comments: 'Some individuals may find comfort from their faith, while others experience a sense of spiritual alienation' (p. 7). The work of Holloway (2005) also offers some very interesting and useful insights into questions of faith and spirituality in 'dark times'.

Our spiritual responses, then, can be equally as significant as the psychological, social and physical ones discussed earlier.

Conclusion

Having considered these five sets of factors that all relate to how grief is experienced by the individual, we should now have a fuller and more telling picture of how wide ranging grief is in its effects. It

Figure 4.2 Spirituality

should also, once again, be clear just how complex grief is as a phenomenon, as a feature of human experience. This is because these five sets of factors will not operate in isolation but will, as we have already seen, interrelate with one another, producing a very subtle and complex, intricate web of factors to be aware of in trying to support someone who is grieving.

In terms of understanding how grief is a healing process, we should be able to see from the discussions in this chapter that this occurs at different levels, particularly the five different levels indicated here. In order to be well placed to support somebody who is grieving, we therefore need to wear their moccasins, as it were, to be able to have a degree of empathy that enables us to appreciate – at these five different but interconnected levels – the impact that grief is having on this person's life. This gives us an important platform of understanding which goes beyond general theories of grief and loss – important though those are – to enable us to 'tune in' to some of the specific issues that will relate to how grief is lived by a real person going through the very painful and often distressing process of grieving. Grief is indeed a form of healing that can have positive results but, of course, that does not alter the fact that it can be an exhausting and painful experience of searing intensity. We have to be sensitive to this in forming the picture of the grieving person's experience, so that we are well informed enough to be able to help and support them in a constructive way.

POINTS TO PONDER

- Why is it important to understand that grief is not just an *emotional* reaction to loss?
- What physical effects of grieving have you experienced at times of loss in your life?
- In what ways is spirituality relevant to loss and grief?

Key texts

1. Dickenson, D., Johnson, M. and Katz, J. S. (eds.) (2000) *Death, Dying and Bereavement*, London, Sage.
2. Hooyman, N. R. and Kramer, B. J. (2006) *Living Through Loss: Interventions Across the Lifespan*, New York, Columbia University Press.
3. Walter, C. A. and McCoyd, J. L. M. (2009) *Grief and Loss Across the Lifespan: A Biopsychosocial Perspective*, New York, Springer.

5

Responding to Grief I: the personal response

Introduction

This is the first of two chapters that examine the way we, as helpers, respond to someone else's experiences of grief. In this particular chapter, the focus is on our own personal reactions – that is, how other people's grief can reawaken our own experiences of loss and can also raise strong feelings of anxiety or even fear. This reflects the quotation from Moss (2007a) in the previous chapter in which he comments on the importance of being aware of how dealing with other people's pain and suffering can have significant echoes of our own such experiences.

If we are to be able to be effective in helping other people deal with the maelstrom of their feelings, then we need to be able to deal with our own feelings. The concept of emotional intelligence is used (but not in an uncritical way) as a foundation for understanding the emotional demands involved. The main emphasis is on how it is important for us, as professional helpers, to be 'in touch' with our own feelings of loss and grief, so that these do not get in the way of our being able to help others cope with their losses. We begin by trying to understand grief as a universal phenomenon.

Universal grief

Of course, it goes without saying that no one is immune from grief. Everyone at some time in their life will experience grief. It is in effect part and parcel of human existence. So, what we are talking about, then, is a case of *when* people experience grief, not *if*. This applies to us as professional helpers as much as it does to the people we are trying to help, so, to use a phrase associated with the work of Nouwen (1996), we are all wounded healers. We all have our own experiences of grief that we carry with us. This means that it is important to use the notion of 'use of self'. The main implication of this is that, as helpers, we should not simply be technicians trying to 'fix' people's problems. Rather, we should see ourselves as human beings encountering other human beings in what can, it is to be hoped, be a positive process of help and support. The basic idea is that helping comes from authentic relationships. As Hamer (2006) puts it:

> It has been shown time and again that the most therapeutic part of any therapeutic relationship is the relationship itself. Not the stuff that is done, not the therapies, but the interaction between two human beings.

> *The gift you offer another person is just your being,*
> Ram Dass

> You can make people feel respected, worthwhile and hopeful, you can build trust from the very moment you meet with them. (p. 12)

This links closely to the work of Buber who, as long ago as 1923 wrote about differences between I-Thou and I-it (Buber, 2004). By the term 'I-Thou' what he meant was relationships based on mutual respect, where each party treats the other in a dignified and constructive way. The result of an I-Thou relationship is the reaffirmation of the humanity of both parties. An I-it relationship by contrast is one where one person treats the other as if they were a thing – perhaps just seeing them as another case, another difficulty to be resolved, or another statistic to be logged – and does not really engage with that person *as a person*. What is particularly significant here, according to Buber, is that this not only dehumanizes the person who is being treated in this way, but it also dehumanizes the person behaving in that way. That is something that we clearly need to avoid at any time in our work in the helping professions, but it is especially significant at a time of intense vulnerability and suffering, as experienced in relation to a major loss and the grief reactions that ensue from it.

PRACTICE FOCUS 5.1

Diane was a social worker in a hospital. Her work mainly involved working with older people to help them make discharge arrangements to ensure that they would be safe and adequately cared for once they got home. Much of the time the referrals came thick and fast and made it a very pressurized job for her. She tried to do her best in difficult circum-stances. However, she was shocked one day to find that one family had made a complaint about her and the way she had managed the case of Mrs Snell. They wrote to the hospital manager to complain that Diane had been 'unfeeling' in dealing with the strong sense of grief they experi-enced in realizing that Mrs Snell would not be able to do many of the things she was able to do before she had a stroke. Diane was horrified to realize that the family felt she had been 'unfeeling'. Their letter said that she had treated them in a very routine way and seemed oblivious to how significant an impact Mrs Snell's stroke would have on them and, of course, on Mrs Snell herself. She began to wonder whether the pres-sures of her work had led her to work with this family in more of a routinized way than she would have liked. This unfortunate situation gave her a lot of food for thought about how she could manage such a high workload without slipping into routinized or mechanistic ways of working.

Because we are all prone to having experiences of grief, we need to recognize that there are two sets of issues that we should consider: present and past. The first of these relates to current grief issues where applicable. That is, where we are experiencing our own grief at any particular time, while also trying to help other people cope with their grief, we need to be very tuned in to the complexi-ties involved. In particular, we need to be careful not to cross profes-sional boundaries. It is very easy for someone who is grieving to encounter someone else who is grieving and for this situation then to develop into a mutual support arrangement. We have to question how appropriate that is in the context of professional roles and boundaries. This is not to say that a professional who is grieving cannot gain some sense of comfort from engaging with other people who are also grieving, and achieve some sense of connectedness or solidarity, but that has to be done within the context of a professional – and not a personal – relationship. We are required to be, after all, friendly professionals, rather than simply friends.

Similarly, it is important to note that, while we are experiencing a significant grief reaction ourselves, we may find ourselves in a strong position to help someone else. It is to be hoped that, as well-informed professionals, we will be sensitive to, and well informed about, grief issues anyway, but this should be especially the case where we are experiencing a grief reaction ourselves. If this does occur, then we can be very helpful towards others, but we should also recognize our own possible need for support and, if the loss reaction is sufficiently intense, then it may be that we have to with-draw ourselves temporarily from working with other people who are grieving, or at least limit our exposure to such matters at a key time. This is something that needs careful judgement, and, again, it may be helpful to seek support on this, in view of the fact that, at a time of your own personal vulnerability, you may not be the best placed person to make a decision about the wisdom or otherwise of responding to someone else's intense grief when you yourself are grieving. Clearly, these are complex and sensitive issues, and so they have to be weighed up very carefully (see Papadatou, 2009, for an extended discussion of the issues relating to 'caring for the carers').

Voice of experience 5.1

❝When my father died I found my work at the hospice actually helped me. Being with people who understood situations like that made me feel supported. But it was a different story when my mother died. For the first few days I couldn't bear to go to work at all, and then for a couple of weeks after that I was on 'light duties', mainly admin work that didn't bring me into contact with people's pain. It was partly because I was closer to my mother than to my father and partly because, well, it was a different situation; it just felt different.**❞**

Selima, a hospice volunteer

The second consideration is what could be called 'opening old wounds'. By this I mean situations where you may not be currently in the throes of significant grief but, by engaging with somebody who is grieving, you may find that this, to use Stroebe and Schut's (1999) terminology, puts you into loss orientation – temporarily at least. That is, by being exposed to someone else's intense pain, you are reminded of your own previous experiences, which can then bring recollections of them back to your mind quite firmly and vividly, for a while at least. This can be especially the case when there is some point of similarity between your own particular loss in the past and the circumstances of the loss for the person that you are currently trying to support. This would be an example of the concept of transference, where aspects of one situation are transferred to another. So, for example, if you meet a person for the first time who reminds you of somebody you like, you may find that you take an instant liking to this person (or if they remind you of someone you do not like, you may find yourself taking an instant dislike to them). So, in parallel fashion, if for example you lost somebody in a car accident, then working with somebody who is grieving for their loved one who also happened to die in a car accident, may create significant issues for you to consider or perhaps even to wrestle with emotionally.

If this is the case, then the same considerations as outlined above (in terms of current grief issues) would need to be taken into account. That is, if the reaction is strong enough, you may not be sufficiently well equipped to help this person currently. In such circumstances, it may be better if you were to withdraw and allow somebody else to try and help, somebody who is better placed to deal with the issues at present. However, if you are able to cope with the demands of this situation without the quality of your practice suffering, and without your suffering as a human being in your own right, then you may well be able to continue to work in this way and to bring a great deal of sensitivity to the issues.

Emotional intelligence

This is a term that is now widely used after being popularized by the work of Goleman (1996). The basic idea behind emotional intelligence is that, as we grow up, we develop the ability to deal with emotions to a significant level of competence. Just as we have a general intelligence which allows us to understand issues at a broader level, the idea of emotional intelligence is that we have a good understanding of how emotions work in human life. The idea has been criticized for being too simplistic and for being 'commodified' (Fineman, 2000). That is, it has been criticized for being something that has produced a bandwagon effect, where very many people have tried to earn a living from selling solutions to emotional intelligence problems and/or developing methods of measuring emotional intelligence or 'EQ', as it has come to be called. However, despite these criticisms, there is still much to be learned about how people respond to emotional issues. This can be understood at two levels: dealing with their own feelings and responding to other people's feelings. Let us look at each of these in turn.

A key part of emotional intelligence is the ability to recognize and respond to other people's feelings. This means having the sensitivity to pick up on nonverbal cues – for example, to recognize the signs that are given off when somebody is experiencing a particular emotion. So, what is involved is the ability to develop the skills and sensitivity needed for tuning into a person's feelings, how they are being expressed and perhaps also why they are being expressed – that is, trying to understand the context in which this emotion is being expressed. This is something that people generally learn – up to a point at least – as part of their upbringing, but many people are very limited when it comes to such sensitivity, and for some, it seems as though it has passed them by completely.

Either way, there is the potential to improve on this: somebody who is already reasonably good at tuning in to emotional issues can take that to a higher, more advanced level, and become quite an expert in doing so. Someone who is not so adept at this type of thing can, though, learn how to do so. In other words, emotional intelligence is a set of skills, rather than a quality that you either have or do not have. People can learn to pick up on the signs of a particular emotion being to the fore in somebody's life at a particular time. This is likely to be particularly significant in relation to grief because, as we noted earlier, there will be a wide range of feelings associated with grief.

PRACTICE FOCUS 5.2

Jim was a trainee psychologist working in a specialist psychiatric unit for adolescents. To begin with he felt a little overwhelmed by the intensity of emotion he encountered there. However, once he started to settle, he felt more comfortable, confident that he was getting better at recognizing – and dealing with – the range of emotions that was so common there. He became fascinated with the topic of human emotion and read widely on the subject. From this reading he began to draw links and form patterns across the range of emotions. Before too long he began to realize that an important linking theme was that of grief. As he worked his way through the files of the young people he was working with he was starting to see to what extent loss featured. He was very surprised at first to note just how many losses most of them had experienced, but it all started to fall into place; it all started to make sense when he began to see the emotional reactions that were so common as features of young lives that were characterized by such breadth and depth of immense loss.

An effective practitioner will therefore be one who is able to tune into these emotions and also make links between the emotions encountered and any underlying grief reaction. For example, in the majority of cases it does not take a great deal of emotional intelligence to recognize when somebody is angry, but many people may not realize that this could be a response to a loss. They may feel that it is just somebody who is behaving in an inappropriate way and thereby become judgemental towards them. This, of course, is not likely to be helpful, and can add to a person's distress rather than alleviate it. It is for this reason, among others, that recognizing, and responding to, other people's feelings is a key ability for professional helpers who are working with people who are grieving or who are traumatized in some way.

The other side of the emotional intelligence coin is recognizing, and responding to, our own feelings. This fits well with my comments earlier about universal grief and how we will all bring to any practice situations our own experience of current or past losses. However, it is not just this that we need to take into consideration. There is also the broader range of emotions that can come into play when we are interacting with other people, especially in those circumstances characterized by intense emotion and feelings of vulnerability. We therefore need to be able to tune into our own feelings, to be aware of how *we* are responding. For example, if we feel insecure as a result of being exposed to some fairly raw emotion, then we need to be aware of that sense of vulnerability, and, moreover, be able to deal with it constructively – rather than allow that vulnerability to prevent us from helping the person we are engaging with.

These are very significant issues, because the price we pay for getting this wrong can be quite high. This applies in two ways. It can be a high price for the person we are trying to help, in so far as they may not get the help they need if our own feelings, our own emotional responses to the situation, get in the way of our being able to help them constructively and positively. Also, though, we need to consider how, as it were, we may lose out as a result of our feelings getting the better of us in such situations. We may experience a degree of distress at the time or later, and may also have a sense of guilt and feel that we have let ourselves down as well as letting down the person we are trying to help if we have not responded to the situation as skilfully as we could have done. This, then, brings us back to the notion of emotional intelligence as a set of skills, lessons that we can learn, rather than something that we either have or do not have from the outset.

There is therefore a significant challenge to us as professional helpers to develop emotional intelligence skills. As I mentioned earlier, if we already have them, then we can look at how we can develop them to a higher level. If we struggle with such issues, then we need to look carefully at what support we need to be able to be better equipped to address the emotional challenges we are likely to encounter in our work. As Corr, Nabe and Corr (2008) comment:

> Good helpers need to evaluate their own strengths and weaknesses ... as well as being open to suggestions and support from other persons – even from the dying person or the family they are helping. Indeed, when dying persons are freed from the burden of distressing symptoms and made to feel secure, they can often be very thoughtful and sensitive in caring for those around them. In short, none of us is without needs in coping with someone else's mortality or with our own mortality. We can all benefit from help as we look to our own tasks in coping. (p. 169)

This links well with the important concept of self-care, a topic that we will explore below.

However, before leaving the topic of emotional intelligence, it is worth mentioning the related concept of spiritual intelligence (Zohar and Marshall, 2000, 2004). This refers to the idea that people need to find meaning in their lives, that we all engage in processes that produce a sense of coherence to our lives. Given the importance of meaning making in response to grief (Attig, 2000; Neimeyer, 2001), this can be seen as an important extension of the idea of emotional intelligence (Moss, 2007b).

Voice of experience 5.2

❝I had various jobs before I came into hospice work but I didn't get any real satisfaction from them; they all seemed fairly empty and meaningless and I was just going through the motions. The work I do now is by far the most demanding type of job I have ever done, but it's also the most rewarding. I can't see me doing any other type of work in future.**❞**

Bernadette, a hospice nurse

Self-care

In an insightful piece of writing Renzenbrink (2004) introduces what I regard as a key concept, that of 'relentless self-care'. She explains:

Several years ago, Robert Hockley, a valued Australian friend and colleague in the loss and grief field, died of cancer in his early fifties. Because we were living on different continents while he was dying, he wrote me a farewell letter. In it he urged me to practice 'relentless self-care,' for he felt that those of us who work with dying and bereaved people are extremely vulnerable to stress and illness and therefore need to take better care of ourselves. (p. 848)

This is not only an important argument in relation to working in the bereavement field, but also one that can be extended to working with loss and grief more broadly – for example, in working with children and young people who have been abused or have experienced a succession of placements that have broken down.

Self-care needs to be relentless, in the sense that it is not something that we can afford to let slip. The price for that would be too high, as the harm that can be done to people involved in this field can be immense – for example, in terms of secondary or 'vicarious' trauma (Harvey, 2002); burnout (Maslach, 1982); and compassion fatigue (Figley, 1999); as well as the broader social impact of strain on relationships, obstacles to career progression and a general negative impact on well-being.

One very important consideration to bear in mind is the question that was raised earlier about whether you are able to deal with a grief-related situation if you are currently wrestling with your own grief issues. So, depending on the seriousness of the situation, when it comes to self-care, one important question to ask yourself is: are you 'fit for work'? If not, it can be dangerous for both the helper and the helped. It is therefore important to know your limitations. It is not a matter of being 'macho' and pressing on regardless. It is something that we need to be aware of, and, of course, it is nothing to be ashamed of (and certainly not a sign of weakness) to be able to say at times that we are not able to undertake certain grief-related tasks. In fact, it can be seen that this is a sign of strength, a sign of emotional awareness that is something to be valued rather than seen as any sort of inadequacy.

But even in situations where we do not have grief issues that are currently to the fore in our lives, we still need to think about coping strategies. This will depend on the nature of your work. For some people (hospice workers, for example) dealing with grief will be a daily occurrence, more or less, and so the coping strategies such people need will have to be fairly well developed if they are going to be able to deal effectively with the emotional pressures of their work on an ongoing basis. If your work is not so directly focused on loss and grief, but you are none the less likely to come into contact with people grieving on a fairly regular basis, then your coping strategies do not need to be so well developed, but you will still need coping strategies of some description. You will need to be able to work out how you cope with the difficulties presented by being exposed to a high level of emotion on an extended basis in some cases.

One such coping strategy is what is known as 'compartmentalization'. This means making sure that, when you are at work, you are focusing on your work pressures and you do not allow home-related pressures to impinge on that. Similarly, when you are at home, you focus on your home pressures and do not allow work-related pressures to impinge on you there. The best-case scenario is one of optimal compartmentalization where you are successfully able to keep the two sets of pressures separate, and thereby maintain an excellent work-life balance. However, the worst-case scenario is where, at work you are focusing on both work and home pressures at the same time, and then taking those work pressures home with you to worry about alongside your home pressures, with the potentially disastrous result that you never have a break from one set of pressures or the other. Developing the skills of compartmentalization is therefore an important part of self-care. Some people facilitate this through some sort of ritual. For example, when they get home from work, they change their clothes or have a shower or do something that, in some way, signals the transition from one set of pressures to another. Compartmentalization can be a difficult skill to develop at first, but it is certainly well worth the effort to do so.

However, compartmentalization on its own will not be enough. We also need to look at other ways of coping, and these will vary from individual to individual. Consequently, what can be useful is for you to think about what sort of things you normally find helpful if you are facing a difficult or demanding situation. For example, some people find it helpful to talk it over with someone else, while others prefer not to do so – they find that talking about such matters makes them experience them more intensely. Other people like to write things down; they may keep a log or diary that can help to process the emotions involved in the situation. There is no set way of dealing with such matters. It is a significant challenge, then, for you to find ways of coping that suit you and your particular style.

PRACTICE FOCUS 5.3

Ahmed was an advice worker in a large voluntary organization. He enjoyed his job, but found it quite pressurized, especially when he was working with someone who was upset or grieving. He would take his concerns home with him and found it difficult to put them behind him and relax. At first it was not a significant problem, but over time his pressures were building up and he was feeling less confident about coping with them. However, what made a major difference to him were the lessons he learned after attending a 'Surviving at Work' course that his employers organized for their staff. On the course he learned the importance of having a repertoire of coping skills and methods and the need to use these as key elements of self-care. This learning boosted his confidence and gave him the opportunity to draw up a list of things he could do to take better care of himself and help deal with the pressures that had been building up.

Hamer (2006) makes the important point that we are each responsible for our own self-care and thus morale:

You can survive as a front line professional in this demanding work. You can keep your spirit intact and function holistically and authentically, but the responsibility for that is yours. You need to look after your spirit and your emotions. Nobody will do it for you. Nobody will even notice or care that you are not coping until it is too late. You have to take responsibility for these things yourself. (p. 52)

This is fair comment but, despite self-care being our own personal responsibility at one level, it is also a shared responsibility. Your employers, under the health and safety legislation, have a responsibility to help protect you from undue hazards, and the stresses of dealing with raw emotion over an extended period of time can clearly be seen to come into that category. So what is worth considering is: what support does your employer offer and how can you make the best use of that support? It is vitally important that we have an open attitude towards such matters and not have a macho approach or a stoic attitude that is based on the dangerous idea that, as robust professionals, we should be able to cope with whatever is thrown at us without the need for support. That sort of assumption is potentially very dangerous. What is much more helpful and positive is to accept that, as human beings dealing with some of the most demanding and challenging aspects of being human, we are, of course, going to need support. It can be helpful to divide that support into two categories: formal and informal. As I have already mentioned, there will be support from our employers; what might be called formal or institutional support, but alongside that there will also be informal support. This refers to the sort of support we may get from colleagues, friends, neighbours and our own family, and so on – various ways in which we can get some sort of sustenance, as it were, from our relationships and our social network (what these days is often referred to as 'social capital' – Castiglione, van Deth and Wolleb, 2008; Lin, 2001).

Self-care, then, is an important subject that should not be neglected or swept under the carpet. What we are doing in responding to other people's grief is placing ourselves in a very difficult position. We have to be realistic about the demands of that. This does not mean, on the one hand, over-reacting and panicking, and assuming that we cannot do it, but we should also avoid the other extreme of being complacent and assuming that we can cope with whatever comes our way without any sort of planning around coping methods and external support. This, then, raises some very important questions that we need to address if we are to be the most effective helpers we can in responding to these major challenges.

Voice of experience 5.3

❝I have seen the effects of people not taking the trouble to do self-care, people who are very strongly committed to giving their all to their work, but who don't leave enough over for themselves. As I have had to say to so many people over the years: if you don't look after yourself you are going to be in no position to look after others.❞

Carwyn, an occupational health nurse

Conclusion

In this the first of two chapters to explore how we respond as effectively as possible to someone else's experiences of grief, we have focused on our own personal responses. We have examined how there are some very significant issues in terms of what we need to do if we are grieving at any particular moment, and what also needs to happen if a situation brings to the fore previous experiences of loss. We have also looked at the importance of emotional intelligence. If we are to be able to cope with the emotional pressures of working in grief-saturated situations, then we need to be able not only to recognize and respond to other people's emotional expressions, but also to recognize and respond appropriately to our own feelings. Linked to this has been the key notion of self-care. While dealing with grief situations may not have the dangers of some jobs (working on high scaffolds, for example) there are none the less significant risks involved. Working with grief is very psychologically draining, and, if we are not careful, our work can do significant harm to us as well as leading to difficulties in helping the people who may be relying on us for support. It is therefore vitally important that, in working with people who are grieving, we take account of our *personal* response to the situation, and not just our professional response. While, as mentioned earlier, we should not be crossing professional boundaries, we none the less have to recognize that we are human beings who are faced with dealing with some of the most intense and demanding aspects of what it means to be a human being.

> **POINTS TO PONDER**
>
> - Are you clear about who could give you support if you needed it as a result of grieving one or more losses?
> - What steps could you take to improve your emotional intelligence?
> - What are your strengths and weaknesses in relation to self-care? How can you build on the former and address the latter?

Key texts

1. Figley, C. (ed.) (1995) *Compassion Fatigue: Coping with Secondary Traumatic Stress Disorder in Those who Treat the Traumatized,* New York, Brunner-Mazel.
2. Papatadou, D. (2009) *In the Face of Death: Professionals who Care for the Dying and the Bereaved*, New York, Springer.
3. Renzenbrink, I. (2011) *Caregiver Stress and Staff Support in Illness, Dying and Bereavement*, Oxford, Oxford University Press.

6

Responding to Grief II: the professional response

Introduction

Chapter 5 was based on the idea that, when we respond to grief situations we do so as human beings in our own right with our own history of losses and potentially our own current grief issues to wrestle with. It is inevitable that we will bring with us our own personal issues, but it is not inevitable that we fail to keep those in perspective or make the mistake of crossing professional boundaries. This chapter now takes these issues a step further, but, by looking at the other side of the coin, it explores the range of ways in which professionals can be helpful and supportive *as professionals*. It therefore complements well the discussions in Chapter 5 about our personal responses: to offer the best level of help and support we can, we need to be able to understand the issues that relate to both our personal and professional responses to grief.

This chapter warns against the simplistic notion that grief counselling is a panacea for dealing with the problems grief raises. I argue here for a much broader psychosocial and spiritual understanding of what is required to be genuinely helpful in supporting people through grief. A key argument is that we cannot take away the pain, and we should not try to, as such futile attempts can make matters worse – for example, by giving the grieving individual the message that we are, at best, lacking in understanding of grief and, at worst, devaluing their feelings by not respecting them, not giving them the consideration they deserve.

In this chapter, then, my focus will be on the various aspects of the professional response to helping somebody on their grief journey

– that is, the various ways in which, as professionals, we can reach out to grieving people in supportive and meaningful ways. It is divided into four parts (being there; assessing and managing risk; practical help; and healing), with each one focusing on a particular aspect of the professional helping response.

Being there

It may sound trite, but one of the most helpful things we can do when somebody is grieving is to be there with them, to have a human presence. This is particularly the case in the early stages of a person's finding out about a loss. They may be so bewildered and overwhelmed by the loss that it will not have 'sunk in' yet, and they will not be in a position to listen to what we have to say or to receive any direct help. However, the fact that we are there can be very significant, both then and at a later stage in the helping process when they may feel very grateful to us for the fact that we stuck with them through what could well have been a very painful, difficult and embarrassing experience for both parties.

A key part of 'being there' is *listening*. We need to be able to hear what people have to say, while resisting the temptation to switch from listening mode to telling mode. Giving people advice or helping to find solutions is unlikely to be helpful in the early stages of the process. What we need to do is to be a human presence, to connect with that person in a meaningful way, and that means that our primary emphasis must be on listening.

Ironically, part of that listening may be enduring silence. If the grieving person has nothing to say, then we have to respect that, because that in itself can be an important part of the healing process, to be able to sit in silence with someone else present who is not trying to dominate, who is not trying to take the situation in their direction, but is just there for them. The therapeutic value of that can be immense. However, it has to be recognized that, particularly for inexperienced professionals, this can be something that is very difficult to do. There can be a huge pressure to fill the gap, to end the silence in whatever way, but we have to read these situations

---

> PRACTICE FOCUS 6.1
>
> Phil was a social worker in a children and families support team. One day he was talking to Terri whose two young children had been removed and placed with foster carers because of major concerns about physical abuse on the part of Terri's partner, Ray. Terri was telling Phil how dreadful she felt about what had happened, how bereft she felt as a result of the losses involved in having her children taken away. Phil was very aware of the acute pain she was experiencing and kept suggesting ways of helping, possible solutions to the difficulties Terri was describing. Terri did not respond to any of Phil's suggestions until she reached the point where she could put up with advice giving no longer. She became angry and, in raised tones, said to him: 'I don't want you to give me advice; I just want somebody to listen'. This sharp retort helped Phil to learn that there are times for helping people in direct, problem-solving ways, and that there are times when all that is needed is to listen. In a sense, listening is the solution to the problem of needing to be listened to. Phil hoped that he would remember this lesson, as his faux pas had made a difficult situation even harder.

very carefully and, if we do have something to say, to make sure that we say it at the appropriate time and not just because we feel uncomfortable about a silence.

A useful concept in relation to listening is that of *dadirri*, a concept deriving from the wisdom of Australian Aboriginal peoples which refers to 'deep' listening (Atkinson, 2002). It involves making a real connection with people. Tehan (2007) refers to it as 'listening with discernment'. She goes on to quote Ungenmerr-Bauman (1988, p. 1):

> [Dadirri] recognizes the deep spring that is inside us. It is something like what you call contemplation … The contemplative way of dadirri spreads over our whole life. It renews us and brings us peace. It makes us feel whole again. In our Aboriginal way we learnt to listen from our earliest times. We could not live good and useful lives unless we listened. We are not threatened by silence. We are completely at home in it. Our Aboriginal way has taught us to be still and wait … when a relation dies we wait for

a long time with the sorrow. We own our grief and allow it to heal slowly. We wait for the right time for our ceremonies and meetings. The right people must be present. Careful presentations must be made. We don't mind waiting because we want things to be done with care … We don't worry. We know that in time and in the spirit of dadirri [that deep listening and quiet stillness] the way will be made clear … We have learnt to speak the white man's language; we have listened to what he had to say. This listening and learning should go both ways. We are hoping people will come closer. We keep longing for the things that we have always hoped for, respect and understanding. (p. 215)

This is a way of connecting with people that can be of benefit across the helping professions in any of our endeavours that involve communicating effectively with people. However, we can also see that it is particularly valuable as a component of our efforts to work with people who are grieving.

To accompany the listening we may sometimes want to offer reassurance. This can be very helpful if done carefully and tactfully and not overdone. We also have to make sure that we are not offering false reassurance – for example, saying something like: 'Everything will be OK' is a risky undertaking, because everything may well not be 'OK'. If the grieving person sees through this, they may become angry and feel that we are not being supportive of them – and that can be counterproductive all round. However, there may be future problems that we are storing up for ourselves by offering false reassurance. For example, if something does not work out as we said it would, then this may be held against us at a later date. We may find ourselves being blamed (this may even form the basis of a complaint) because we made false promises, we gave false reassurances.

Where the grief is in relation to a loss that is not death related, we may need to help them recognize that it is none the less a loss situation that they are in (that in itself can be a major way of helping at times). Because of the tendency to associate loss and grief primarily, if not exclusively, with bereavement, the fact that, in certain situations, nobody has died is likely to mean that people do not identify it as a loss situation. They do not realize that they are going through a grief reaction. It can therefore be an important role for the professional helper to assist the grieving person in realizing that they are in fact grieving, and that this is a legitimate response to a loss, even where that loss is not an actual bereavement.

As mentioned above, one other vitally important factor to consider is that we cannot take the pain away from a grieving person; nor should we try. It is futile to try and turn a situation involving grieving into one that is pain free. We are trying to do the impossible. Not only is that a waste of time and effort, but it can also be counterproductive. This is because we can be giving the grieving person two unhelpful messages. The first unhelpful message is one that says: 'I am trying to help you through grief but I don't really understand grief because, if I did have an understanding of grief, I would not try to take the pain away. I would not try to do the impossible.' The second unhelpful message is that you are devaluing their pain; you are failing to appreciate the significance of it. It may be seen that you are at best failing to understand and, at worst, trivializing something that, at that particular moment, is a crucial factor to that person.

Voice of experience 6.1

❝One of the most difficult lessons I have learned in my time in this job is that, when people are grieving, I cannot make it all better for them. Even now, after six years of practice, I still have to resist the temptation to try and take the pain away and to make sure I do my real job of helping them on that painful journey.❞

Cassie, a counsellor

Clearly, then, we have to move away from any attempts to try and take the pain away. This comes back to the discussions in the previous chapter about our own personal responses to loss. It may be that, in trying to take the pain away, we are dealing with our own feelings; that we are trying to make ourselves feel more comfortable, because it can be very difficult – excruciating even – to bear witness to someone going through the intense pain and suffering of a major loss. However, this is precisely what we need to do – bear witness – rather than try to do the impossible. In fact, this is what 'being there' is all about: bearing witness, being an important fellow passenger on one of the most difficult journeys people will take in their lives.

A key concept in terms of being there is that of 'human communion'. This relates back to our earlier discussions of spiritual connectedness, the importance of being able to connect in meaningful ways with other human beings, to have a sense of solidarity and being part of a wider whole. That helps to take away some of the feelings of isolation and alienation that are characteristic of a grief reaction. This is then closely related to the idea of security, particularly ontological security, as discussed earlier. By being there with people, being part of this connectedness, we are helping to create a sense of security to counteract the intense insecurity and vulnerability that is so much part and parcel of a grief reaction. It is therefore important, particularly in the early stages of helping, to make sure that we are not trying to provide technical fixes. There is a role for problem-solving activities, but this is likely to be at a later stage in the process as we shall see below. In the early stages, though, being there is the primary concern, helping to create that sense of connectedness to reduce the sense of insecurity and vulnerability, to help create a stronger foundation of ontological security.

One of the most important things we need to bear in mind in terms of helping this way is the balance of giving support and giving people space. We will want to be helpful in whatever ways we reasonably can, but we also need to recognize that the grieving person will need some personal space, to feel that they have support, but also that they are not hemmed in by that support. We therefore need a great deal of sensitivity in relation to such matters, and this is where the emotional intelligence we discussed in Chapter 5 comes to the fore: being able to read the situation in ways that allow us to offer that appropriate balance of support and personal space.

In situations that involve 'being there', it is not uncommon – particularly for inexperienced helpers – to come away from such situations feeling hopeless and helpless, feeling that we have not been able to contribute, that we have not been able to do anything positive. However, this is a feeling that we need to challenge and displace because the reality is: being there is one of the most helpful things we can possibly do. Being able to cope with our own wish to 'make it all better' and take the pain away is one of the most important sets of skills that we can develop as professional helpers. This is one of the main reasons why dealing with our own personal response to somebody else's grief was given a whole chapter in its own right – such is its importance.

Assessing and managing risk

Unfortunately, in recent years, we have seen a movement in the direction of professional helpers becoming more risk averse – that is, moving in the direction of being far less likely to allow risks to exist (Denney, 2005; Swift and Callahan, 2009; Thompson, 2009c). This can be very counterproductive for two reasons. The first reason is that we are setting ourselves up to fail if we feel that we can produce risk-free situations. Human existence, by its very nature, involves sets of risks and, if we try to remove one set of risks, we are just creating a different set of risks and those risks may, in fact, be worse. That links in very well with my second point about being risk averse, which is that, in doing so, we may actually be behaving in an oppressive way. Risk-taking behaviours are often the source of a person's identity, their self-esteem, and so on. Therefore, trying to remove such risk factors can be very harmful (as a result of introducing another set of perhaps worse risks as well as being oppressive and disempowering in its own right). Consequently, in considering the question of risk, we have to be conscious of the fact that there has been a distinct move in the direction of being risk averse (if not, in some cases at least, actually paranoid about risk).

Grief brings about considerable vulnerability and, where there is vulnerability, there is risk. We therefore need to take every reasonable precaution we can to make sure that these risks do not produce further harmful situations. It can be helpful to break this down into three component parts:

- *Risk to self.* In some situations, there can be a very strongly irrational reaction to a loss that can result in self-harming behaviours, even to the point of suicide attempts. There can also be a strong risk of depression as a result of a major loss. A further set of risks to self relates to the medical conditions that a person may have. For example, as mentioned in Chapter 4, if somebody has a heart condition, then the further stress of grief can produce a potentially life-threatening situation. There are, then, some important considerations in relation to self in relation to how the grieving person may potentially experience harm as a result of the risk factors involved.
- *Risk to others.* The point was made earlier that grief can sometimes be directed outwardly as anger or even aggression. What can happen, then, is that, in some circumstances a grieving person may become verbally abusive towards another person; may become aggressive or even violent; and, in some circumstances, may behave in entirely inappropriate ways towards others – ways that would not normally be characteristic of their behaviour, but which are reflections of the emotional maelstrom that they are currently going through.
- *Risk from others.* When a person is vulnerable as the result of a major loss, they can be open to exploitation or even abuse at the hands of unscrupulous people. For example, it is not uncommon in certain quarters for people who are grieving to be financially exploited, whether by people they know or by people who call at their house on the pretext of trying to sell them a product or a service. This sort of 'scam' can create immense difficulties for a grieving person who then has to contend with the additional pressures of dealing with such a situation.

The third category could also encompass situations where grieving individuals are placed at risk as a result of the interventions of professionals who are not tuned into the significance of grief or have little understanding of how it can affect people. Ill-informed or misguided professional interventions are therefore part of the risk scenario that we need to take into consideration. This is, among other things, a strong argument for the inclusion of a strong focus on loss and grief in professional education across the helping professions.

In situations where risks are seen to be unacceptably high, there may be a need for advocacy. Depending on the particular role you occupy as a professional helper, it may be that you are the person to offer advocacy directly as part of your job, or it may be more appropriate for you to make a referral to a suitable advocacy source to get the help that this person needs in order to deal with the risk factors they face – particularly where the risk is from others in terms of the potential for exploitation and abuse.

PRACTICE FOCUS 6.2

Carla was a health visitor in a rural area. She had been visiting Mr and Mrs Jameson, both in their 80s, as Mr Jameson had severe breathing problems as a result of emphysema. She had been informed by the GP that Mr Jameson had died so, when she was next in that area, she called in to express her condolences and to see how Mrs Jameson was faring, as she too was in poor health. Carla was horrified to find that someone from a double-glazing company had pressurized her into taking out a contract for an expensive programme of window replacement. Mrs Jameson explained to Carla that she had become very confused because the sales rep kept going on at her and, in the end, she wasn't a hundred per cent sure what she had signed up for. Fortunately, there was an advocacy scheme for older people in the area and Carla was able to make a referral so that Mrs Jameson could get some much-needed help in trying to get the contract cancelled before it was too late.

In such emotionally charged circumstances, it may sound callous to do a professional risk assessment, but in some circumstances, it may be crucial to do so. We have to remember that our professional role is partly to help someone deal with the emotional challenges they face, but also partly involves having a broader, more holistic perspective on this. This involves recognizing that grief is not simply a psychological phenomenon, and that it has wider implications –

for example, the social implications in terms of the risks presented to self and to other people.

Practical help

This topic serves as a good example of how we need to understand grief as being more than a psychological reaction. There is a very common tendency for people to assume that, if someone is grieving, they need bereavement counselling (or grief counselling, as it is not necessarily a bereavement that has brought about the loss). There are two problems with this assumption. First, there can be a false assumption that a grieving person needs professional help of any description; and, second, if they do need professional help, it can be a significant mistake to assume that the help should be in the form of counselling. Although counselling can be extremely helpful in the right circumstances, in many situations it may be the last thing that people need in their overall list of priorities for help. Consider, for example, the following three areas where help may be needed:

- *Financial help.* If a person loses their partner, they may also lose a significant source of income, and so, in the short term, until financial affairs can be organized, there may be a need for financial assistance of some description. The worry of such matters can be so intense that they add significantly to the emotional pressures arising from the actual grief. We should therefore be careful not to underestimate the significance of financial concerns at a time of significant loss. This is also very relevant when losses are not related to a death – for example, where somebody is laid off or made redundant.
- *Housing.* The loss may be directly related to housing, in the sense that a person may experience a significant grief reaction if they are evicted or otherwise made homeless. But the other side of the coin is that a bereavement may also lead to housing problems. For example, in a situation where a young adult is living with a sole-remaining parent in a tenancy, then the

death of that parent may mean that the young person has no right to remain in that property. At the time of writing, this situation is being reviewed in the UK, as the result of campaigning by housing pressure groups. However, there can be significant concerns and worries around housing, and so offering somebody counselling when the main worry is to do with their housing needs may not be fruitful.

- *Transport.*   Imagine a situation where an elderly couple live together and one of them drives but the other one does not. If they are living in a rural area this can be particularly significant. But, imagine now that the person who drives passes away. This can then leave the grieving survivor with major difficulties in terms of transport, perhaps simply in terms of practicalities like getting shopping and generally getting about. To many people, this is an issue that would not occur to them if they are just focusing stereotypically on the emotional dimension of a grief reaction.

Voice of experience 6.2

❝I really enjoy my work, even though it is very difficult in some ways. I work with the family support team to help grieving relatives to cope with all the practical problems that arise after a death. It can be quite complicated at times. I had never appreciated how many practical issues there are.**❞**
Jean, a hospice volunteer

These are just three among many such sets of practical challenges that a grieving person may face. There can be myriad problems and difficulties because of a loss. This is perhaps because the person who has died was the one who previously organized certain matters or made certain provisions and who is, as a result of death, no longer available to do so. Similar issues can also apply where a loss is not death related – for example, as a result of a divorce or separation as a consequence of somebody being imprisoned. In such circumstances, loss can result in significant feelings of confusion, anxiety and a lack of confidence, resulting in the grieving person having major difficulties in dealing with the social challenges in terms of the practicalities of living their life without the person they had previously relied upon.

There can also be significant issues in terms of practical help in relation to carer issues – for example, if the carer of a disabled person is no longer available to provide that care (because they have died or they have moved out of the situation – perhaps as a result of being admitted to residential care themselves, as is often the case with older people who rely on each other). In such circumstances there may be significant practical arrangements that need to be addressed. These are just some of the examples of where practical help needs to be to the fore. This is not to say that counselling does not have a part to play. In the right circumstances, counselling can offer immensely important help. The danger, though, is adopting an uncritical perspective on such matters and automatically assuming that what a grieving person needs is counselling.

Healing

At various points in the book, I have referred to the process of helping as being one of facilitating healing. Again it is important to emphasize that this is not to be understood in a medical sense in terms of 'getting better', as if grief were some sort of illness or pathology. It is perhaps better understood not as a biological matter, but as a psychosocial and spiritual one. So, healing from this more holistic perspective means being able to come to terms with the challenges that we face – for example, in terms of developing new meanings.

Writing a new narrative helps us make sense of the circumstances we now find ourselves in after our loss (or losses). This is reflected in meaning reconstruction theory (Neimeyer, 2001) and Attig's notion of 'relearning the world' (Attig, 2001, 2011). It also fits well with phenomenological and existentialist approaches which emphasize the importance of meaning making (Tomer, Eliason and Wong, 2008).

From the social point of view, healing refers to reaffirming our place in society, especially in terms of connectedness to other people, our sense of being part of a broader whole and moving away from the profound sense of isolation and alienation that can be characteristic of grief situations. But, perhaps the most important aspect of this holistic perspective on healing is the spiritual dimension. Some people may think it sounds trite to talk of spiritual healing, and many people will no doubt feel cynical about such matters and associate what sounds like a very fanciful notion with new-age, tree-hugging nonsense. However, this would be a mistake because, whether through religion or other forms of spirituality, a high proportion of the population are engaged with spiritual concerns. Spiritual healing is about finding a new path, about being able to get back to a point in our lives where it all made sense and we understood who we are and where we fitted into the wider picture. It is for this reason that grief can be transformational very often, as some people who struggle with those questions in the first place will find that a major loss has helped them to find some meaningful answers. For many people, though, the spiritual quest, as it were, is to re-establish some sense of ontological security, to find a degree of relative security where they no longer feel that sense of vulnerability is a strongly defining feature of their lives.

PRACTICE FOCUS 6.3

Marlon was a community worker in a deprived area on the outskirts of a large city. He found his work interesting and rewarding, although quite challenging at times. However, what proved to be a particularly challenging experience arose when a local factory burned down, killing 17 people and seriously injuring 36 others. He now faced the major challenge of helping a community to deal with a welter of grief issues. He very quickly read up on the subject, as it was not one that he had any previous knowledge of. From his reading he realized that the spiritual dimension was one that would need a great deal of attention. He therefore quickly convened a meeting of representatives from local church groups and set about trying to develop a community plan that would address the spiritual issues involved in trying to come to terms with such a significant loss. He was also aware that the focus would need be on spirituality, rather than religion, as he was aware that many people affected would not be members of faith communities, but would still none the less have spiritual needs.

In terms of helping people with such healing, there are no easy answers, no technical fixes that we can offer. In a sense, it is a matter of incorporating the various issues discussed above – that is: the being there or bearing witness aspect; the assessing and managing risk (in a sense offering a degree of protection for people through very difficult circumstances); and, of course, offering practical help, engaging in problem-solving activities where needed. The combined effect of helping in these various ways is to make a human connection, thereby being in a position to be able to provide a platform for spiritual growth.

Bauman (1991), in his powerful analysis of the Holocaust, reminds us of just how inhuman humanity can be. Our history of wars, strife, genocide, destruction, cruelty and abuse further confirms that, as a species, we are capable of immense atrocities. However, balanced against that, we must recognize that we are also capable of great compassion, acts of immense kindness, warmth and support. It is from these more positive acts that we can take pride and satisfaction, and it is these too that can motivate us to want to help, support and empower other people. When people are fragile and vulnerable because of one or more losses, they are easy prey to cruelty and exploitation, but they are also in a position where they may benefit most from human compassion and connection. It is also at these times that the helper – professional or otherwise – can gain the most satisfaction and reward from being a helper. One flawed, fragile human being (as we indeed all are) helping another flawed, fragile and grieving human being provides us with the basis for meaningful connection and an authentic sense of communion with our fellow travellers on life's journey (Holloway and Moss, 2010).

We also need to recognize that, at times there may be the need for specialist help, particularly when grief is 'complicated' – something we will examine in more detail in Part III.

Conclusion

As we have seen, providing a professional response to people's experiences of loss is a broad undertaking, not just about psychological interventions, such as counselling, but looking more holistically at the wider range of challenges that people face. But, as we have noted, underpinning this is the recognition that we should not assume that professional help is needed, other than perhaps the being there and reassurance and signposting to other more informal sources of help. In this regard the comments of Kellehear (2005) are quite significant:

> Recently two students were shot dead at one of the local universities in my city. I watched the television news coverage of the aftermath and was struck by a reporter's final observations in her report: 'Students and staff at the university are being provided with counselling.' I would like to live in a society where the first words about comfort and healing are recorded in the following way: '… and staff and students are now talking and commiserating with their friends and family.' (p. ix)

Furedi (2004) echoes these sentiments when he criticizes the development of what he calls 'therapy culture', the tendency to assume that personal and social problems are best dealt with by some form of therapeutic intervention.

It is likely that, where professional help will be needed is in those situations where there is a lack of personal or social support – for example, where somebody is isolated (perhaps an elderly person living alone who has no relatives). There will also be situations where there are complicating factors, a range of issues that can make grief an even more difficult challenge to face and these are the sort of issues that we will be addressing in Chapter 7.

Voice of experience 6.3

❝As part of my assessment I have to find out how much support people have by way of friends and family and so on. That then enables me to get some idea of who is likely to need extra support from us in getting through the difficult adjustments involved.**❞**

Calvin, a support worker with a voluntary organization that supports relatives of people who have had a stroke

This, then, concludes Part II. We have looked at grief from the point of view of the grieving person that we are trying to help (Chapter 4), with a view to developing an empathic picture of what is happening, but without falling into the trap of assuming that this person's grief reaction will follow a standard pattern the same as everybody else's. We need to recognize that there will be commonalities, but there will also be factors that are unique to that person. We therefore have to be skilful and patient in tuning into the specifics of that person's lifeworld at that difficult time in their life. This led into our discussions in Chapter 5 about our own personal responses to grief, and a consideration of how it would be naive and potentially disastrous not to take account of the personal impact on us of working with somebody who is going through a significant process of grief. There are no magic answers to this set of challenges, but there are ways in which we can strengthen our robustness and our resilience, so that we are better equipped to be helpful to them without experiencing further pain and suffering ourselves as a result of our own history of loss experiences. In this third and final chapter in Part II, we have switched our focus to the professional response, the various ways in which we can help people to cope with grief where they need some form of professional input. A key message that I want to emphasize by way of conclusion is the importance of recognizing that there are a wide range of helping interventions that we can draw upon, and we should not simply fall into the trap of assuming that there is one given way of helping somebody who is grieving.

POINTS TO PONDER

- How might you deal with your own feelings of discomfort if called upon to simply 'be there' for someone who is grieving?
- What do you see as the most important issues in relation to assessing and managing risk?
- What practical tasks might you be able to undertake to help and accompany someone in their healing?

Key texts

1. Machin, L. (2008) *Working with Loss and Grief*, London, Sage.
2. Thompson, N. (ed.) (2002) *Loss and Grief: A Guide for Human Services Practitioners*, Basingstoke, Palgrave Macmillan.
3. Weinstein, J. (2008) *Working with Loss, Death and Bereavement: A Guide for Social Workers,* London, Sage.

Part III

Grief without healing

Introduction

The point was made earlier that grief can be seen as a positive, if painful and exhausting, journey – a constructive process that helps us make the transition from one part of our life to another, and helps to equip us for facing the demands of the new situation without the person or thing that we have been grieving for. However, there are various ways in which this process can 'go wrong' – it can go awry and create major difficulties for people. This is often referred to as 'complicated grief'. It is where our grief reaction is complicated by a range of problematic factors. In turn, it can also contribute to a wide range of problems, so it is important for us to have a reasonably good understanding of the various ways in which the constructive process of healing that is grief can somehow lead us into situations that are highly problematic.

As with Parts I and II, this part of the book is divided into three chapters. In Chapter 7 we explore the factors that complicate grief. We look at the key question of: what is it that can make such a negative difference to the way a person grieves? In Chapter 8 we explore how grief can lead to psychological problems. That is, in this chapter we focus on the personal reactions to a grief situation that can in some way be challenging and problematic and, in some cases, potentially disastrous. In Chapter 9, we take this a step further and we explore the less well-trodden ground of how grief can contribute to *social* problems. This is something that is often neglected in the literature. The chapter discusses situations in which complications relating to grief can contribute to a range of social problems, such as crime, violence, homelessness and so on.

7

Complications in grieving

Introduction

The idea of 'abnormal' grief, with its pathologizing and judgemental implications, has now largely been superseded by the idea of 'complicated' grief to refer to those situations where additional concerns are encountered. However, even the term 'complicated' grief is problematic to a certain extent, and is therefore far from ideal. This chapter examines the complex issues involved and provides an overview of additional factors that can intensify the difficulties associated with grief, whether the issues are related to the nature of the loss (multiple or cumulative losses), the reaction to the loss (disenfranchised grief, as discussed earlier), or characteristics of the griever (mental health problems, learning disabilities and so on) or their circumstances. However, it is important that we should be aware of the difficulties associated with prescriptive notions of delayed or extended grief. This is because the rate at which a person grieves can differ significantly from the rate at which others grieve and is not necessarily, in itself, a problem or a factor that would lead us to conclude that this merits the title of 'complicated' grief.

As Neimeyer (2000) helpfully explains:

> Although it is important not to 'pathologize' grieving by present-ing it as if it were an illness, it is also important to acknowledge that satisfactory reorganization of one's life following a major loss is not a guaranteed outcome. Indeed, there are several ways we can become 'stuck' in the grief cycle, so that grieving is apparently absent, becomes chronic, or is life-threatening. These negative

outcomes may be more likely when the loss is a traumatic one (involving violation of one's own body, as in rape or physical assault; or a loved one is victimized by violence or senseless killing, as by a drunk driver). (p. 14)

In using the term 'complicated' grief, it is important to recognize that it is a contested notion. Many people would argue that it is not an appropriate term, because all grief is complicated. Indeed, this reflects what has been a message throughout this book: that grief is a complex matter. My own view is that the term 'complicated' grief is not perfectly suited to our needs, but it is the best one we have at present, and is certainly a lot better than the previous notion of 'abnormal' or 'pathological' grief.

In this chapter I will outline various ways in which grief can become complicated and consider some of the implications of this. I will also explore 'vulnerability factors' that can make certain people more prone to complications in grieving; how people often react to grief in ways that make the situation worse; the costs and consequences of complicated grief; and how we can respond to complicated grief and its challenges. However, before embarking on this discussion I will make some brief introductory comments about the significance of pressure and stress in relation to grief in general and complicated grief in particular, as there are important links to be drawn.

Grief, pressure and stress

In an earlier work (Thompson, 2002) I discussed the relationships between grief, pressure and stress. Without revisiting those issues in detail, what is important to note at this point is that grief brings with it additional pressures that can lead to people experiencing stress. This is a relatively straightforward and non-contentious proposition. However, what complicates matters here is that the process can also operate in reverse. That is, if someone is already experiencing stress for whatever reason and then subsequently encounters a major loss, the combination of pressures may prove too much to bear. The consequence of this can be:

- A mental health crisis (a 'nervous breakdown' to use the everyday term);
- Self-harm and/or suicidal thoughts (suicidal ideation, to use the technical term) or even suicide attempts;
- Withdrawal and/or depression;
- High levels of tension that can lead to conflicts and relationship breakdowns.

Each of these can lead to a vicious circle, with one set of pressures adding to other pressures which, in turn, increase the original set of pressures. It is therefore important to recognize that much of what counts as 'complicated' grief arises from a combination of pressures which can lead to a vicious circle (Figure 7.1). The

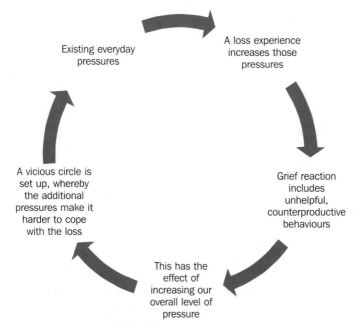

Existing everyday pressures

A loss experience increases those pressures

Grief reaction includes unhelpful, counterproductive behaviours

This has the effect of increasing our overall level of pressure

A vicious circle is set up, whereby the additional pressures make it harder to cope with the loss

Figure 7.1 Grief and pressure

significance of this should become apparent as we explore other aspects of complicated grief.

Before leaving the subject of grief, pressure and stress, it is worth examining how the distinction between pressure and stress can help cast light on the difference between 'ordinary' grief and the 'complicated' variety. Pressure refers to any demands that are made upon us in our everyday lives. Pressure can be positive or negative, depending on the type, amount, duration and intensity of pressure. It can be positive by motivating, stimulating and energizing people. However, it can also be negative when it reaches a level, intensity or duration that causes harm. This can mean harm to health, well-being, confidence, quality and quantity of work, relationships and other aspects of our lives. It is when pressure reaches a level that we struggle to cope with that we define it as stress (Cranwell-Ward and Abbey, 2005; Sutherland and Cooper, 2000; Thompson, 1999).

We can now draw a parallel between this and types of grief. 'Ordinary' grief can be equated with pressure, in the sense that (i) it makes demands on us, but does not necessarily strain our ability to cope with what is involved – it is generally a painful and exhausting process, but most people cope with it most of the time, usually with support from others (Bonanno, 2009); and (ii) there is both a positive and a negative side to it (the positive element being the potential for transformational grief – see Chapter 2). By contrast, complicated grieving (Figure 7.2) can be equated with stress because (i) in such circumstances, our ability to cope becomes strained, sometimes beyond breaking point in which case a crisis is said to have occurred, as also discussed in Chapter 2; and (ii) complicated grief can be seen to do great harm in a high proportion of cases – particularly to people's ability to hold jobs, to sustain relationships and to deal with the everyday challenges they face.

In considering complicated grief, we should therefore bear in mind the important parallels with pressure and stress and the potential for very destructive vicious circles to develop.

Having laid down a foundation that highlights the significance of pressure and stress, we can now move on to consider some of the

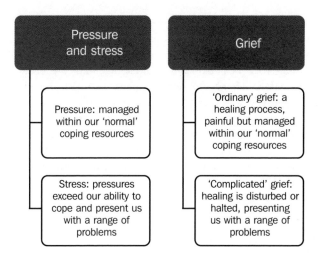

Figure 7.2 Pressure, stress and grief

key factors that can be seen to play a part in making grief experiences complicated and thus problematic.

The nature of the loss experience

As we have noted earlier, loss can take various forms and can occur in various ways. In a similar vein, we can see that there are various factors which can lead to additional problems that complicate the grieving process and which are associated with the nature of the particular loss. We are going to explore four of these in particular.

The first one is the notion of 'cumulative loss'. This refers to situations in which one loss is quickly followed by another and shortly thereafter a further loss, and so on, with the result that, over a relatively short period of time, there can be a series of losses. For some people, this cumulative process can take place over an extended period. Two examples come immediately to mind. One is the situation that a number of older people face when they reach the stage in life where they begin to lose friends through death, and may also be experiencing other losses through disability, for example, or even what might be called symbolic losses (for example, the death of their childhood favourite actor or singer or whatever). A second example would relate to a gay person whose circle of friends has been devastated by AIDS. Thanks to developments in medical technology, being diagnosed as HIV positive is not necessarily a death sentence these days (in the affluent nations at least) but, in the height of the major concerns about AIDS, this was certainly the case for many people who lost key person after key person because of the ravaging effects of AIDS (and continues to be the case in Africa and some other parts of the world).

For some people cumulative loss can occur over a relatively short period of time, as Practice focus 7.1 illustrates.

PRACTICE FOCUS 7.1

Jon was the deputy manager of a day centre for older people. When he found out that Mrs Marsland's husband had died, he realized that he would need to be even more supportive than usual and be sensitive to her grieving. A week later he found out that her sister had been diagnosed with cancer. He was acutely aware of how difficult it must have been for her to deal with this situation when she was already grieving. The next blow came only a few days later when Mrs Marsland was informed that her 25-year-old grandson had been arrested for being in possession of heroin. Jon saw a rapid deterioration in her health and well-being, and, perhaps not surprisingly, she became quite depressed. He became very worried about her and hoped that she would not face another set of losses, as she was clearly already struggling to cope with the recent sequence of events. He wondered how he and the staff team could best help her to get through this really difficult time in her life.

Cumulative losses can leave people punch drunk with grief reaction after grief reaction. The net result of this can be major difficulties in coping, where the individual concerned does not have a chance to begin to 'get over' (or perhaps 'get through' would be a better term) one loss before another one strikes. As the term implies, the effect can then be cumulative. Each new loss adds to the weight of pain and suffering and can potentially produce a situation of paralysis, in which the individual concerned feels unable to address the losses being experienced.

Another important aspect of loss experience is the potential for multiple losses. This is sometimes confused with cumulative loss, but what this term actually refers to is where a number of losses occur *at the same time* – that is, not in sequence, but as a result of one incident or occurrence. For example, an individual may lose several members of their family as a result of a road traffic accident. The net result can be the same as a series of cumulative losses – that is, the individual feeling overwhelmed, not able to cope with the intensity of the loss experience. Again, this can lead to paralysis where the person concerned just does not know where to begin in terms of grieving. It can also relate to other issues that arise as a result of this. We shall return to this point below under the heading 'The effects of complicated grief'.

Multiple losses can also be experienced in situations that do not involve death. For example, a child who is abused can lose trust, security, confidence, identity and, in some respects perhaps, their childhood itself. Similarly, someone who has a mental health crisis could lose their job, their home, a set of relationships, dignity, self-respect, confidence, security and, if admitted to hospital on a compulsory basis, their liberty. It is therefore important not to think too narrowly about what could be seen to constitute a multiple-loss situation.

A third type of loss that often brings additional complications is unexpected loss. We tend to assume that children will be born, will grow up, become adults, become older adults and eventually die, but this general pattern is often broken by unexpected developments. Any major loss can be difficult to deal with, but where the loss is not expected, this can be particularly difficult. This can apply to various situations – for example, where a child is killed, where someone is murdered or, indeed, a wide range of non-death-related losses (for example, somebody who feels they are safe in their job suddenly finding out that they are being laid off, or perhaps someone who is under the impression that there are no major problems with their marital relationship, who suddenly finds that divorce is on the cards).

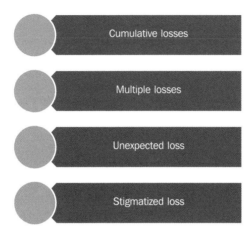

Figure 7.3 Losses that can 'complicate' grief

The fourth type of loss experience that can lead to complications is stigmatized loss. This returns us to the subject of disenfranchised grief, as discussed earlier. Where there is no social recognition of the loss being experienced, then this can bring about additional pressures that can make it harder for the person who is facing grief to deal with the challenges involved. This can be particularly stressful for individuals if it is combined with other issues, such as cumulative, multiple or unexpected losses. However, even without these additional factors, a stigmatized loss can be enough in itself to lead to complications.

In addition to the four sets of complicating factors outlined here and in Figure 7.3, we also need to bear in mind that the nature of the loss experience is also significant where trauma is involved. Where a person has experienced a traumatizing event or process, the result in terms of a grief reaction can be intensified further. For example, consider the type of situation I mentioned above where children are abused. This can have a profound effect on them in terms of their overall well-being. It can lead to situations where the child is experiencing a major grief reaction, but this may actually be disenfranchised if people do not recognize that (i) abuse can be traumatic; and (ii) trauma is closely associated with grief. There is now a growing recognition of the significance of childhood trauma on later adult life (see, for example, Fleming and Belanger, 2001).

Voice of experience 7.1

❝I have worked with abused children for almost seven years now and I have started to see common patterns of trauma during that time. Of course, you have to see each child as a unique individual in their own right and not pre-judge matters, but the effects of trauma are generally clearly there to be seen, just like in the textbooks.**❞**

Carol, a child therapist

Loss itself can be traumatic. As Harvey (2002) comments:

Trauma … refers to a special category of experience connected to loss. When a loss is experienced as traumatic, the loss usually involves some type of sudden, violent death, or the threat of such a death. (p. 2)

Rando (2000a) takes this a step further in identifying six factors that can make a death traumatic:

1. Suddenness and lack of anticipation;
2. Violence, mutilation and destruction;
3. Preventability and/or randomness;
4. Loss of one's child;
5. Multiple deaths; and
6. The mourner's personal encounter secondary to a significant threat to survival and/or shocking confrontation with the death and mutilation of others. (cited in Rando, 2003, p. 266)

However, while Harvey's and Rando's comments are helpful in casting light on death-related traumatic losses, we must be careful not to neglect circumstances that can prove traumatic without death being directly involved. As discussed in Chapter 2, there is a wide range of non-death-related events that can produce a traumatic reaction: being a victim of crime; being abused; witnessing a horrific incident; and so on.

Vulnerability factors

In trying to develop our understanding of complicated grieving, we also need to appreciate the role of 'vulnerability factors'. What I mean by vulnerability factors is the range of things that can have the effect of making us more liable to a complicated form of grief reaction. One of these is a lack of support. Where we have little by way of 'social capital', we can feel isolated, we can feel that we have no support to draw upon, and this can then intensify the sense of hopelessness and helplessness commonly associated with loss and grief. What this can then result in is people who have relatively little by way of a network of social support becoming even more vulnerable to having additional difficulties when it comes to meeting the challenges of grief. As noted earlier, grief brings with it a certain level of stress, and we have known for quite some time now that one of the key factors in responding to stress in general, and grief in particular, is the presence of social support (Miller, 2000; Rowling, 2003).

Linked to this is the significance of mental health problems. People who already have some form of mental difficulty to contend with may really struggle to cope with the additional strains of grief. In fact, one significant factor to consider is that people experiencing mental health problems may be doing so because of unresolved pre-existing grief issues (see Chapter 9 for further discussion of this topic). However, for present purposes, we can note that this is a significant set of factors that can make people more prone to additional difficulties in grieving. If somebody is prone to depression, or is perhaps experiencing difficulties in terms of what is known as bipolar disorder or other such conditions, then the combination of these concerns with the additional difficulties of now facing a grief reaction, may take that particular person beyond the level of pressure they can cope with. This can also be linked to the previous point about a possible lack of social support. It has been recognized for some time now (Sartorius, 2003) that people with mental health problems are often isolated and could potentially benefit from additional social capital.

PRACTICE FOCUS 7.2

Keith was a community psychiatric nurse who had always been interested in grief and its impact on people's lives, influenced no doubt by his mother's role as a hospice nurse. However, it was only when he worked with Daniel, a man with psychotic tendencies who had tried to take his own life, that he realized just how much of an impact grief could have on an individual. Keith was called upon to do an assessment of Daniel's mental state and wider circumstances with a view to helping him avoid reaching the point where he once again felt the need to commit suicide. Keith was surprised at how open Daniel was and how freely he talked about his life experiences. What very quickly became apparent was just how many major losses Daniel had encountered in his life. Even though Keith was quite experienced, he had never realized that someone's life could be characterized by so much grief and actually felt a bit overawed by the stories he was hearing. What particularly struck him was how there had been, on so many occasions in Daniel's life, powerful interactions between his grieving and his mental health problems – with grief triggering off psychotic reactions at times and the difficulties his mental health problems created in turn making it all the more difficult to cope with his grief. It made Keith wonder how many of his other patients had had similar 'loss histories' and how much of a contribution loss had been making to their mental health problems – and how much their mental health problems had perhaps also affected how well or otherwise they coped with their grief.

Another group of people who face particular vulnerability factors are those with learning disabilities. This can be partly as a result of the disability itself. For example, an autistic person may have difficulties understanding what is happening when a loss is experienced, but this is not the only important element of the situation. There can be further vulnerability factors associated with the social response to such a disability: the stigma and discrimination and the stereotypical assumptions that are part and parcel of disablism (Swain et al., 2004).

This leads us into a discussion of one further set of vulnerability factors, namely discrimination itself. Where people are socially marginalized because of racism or any other form of discrimination, then there can be additional factors to consider in relation to this. The work of Barrett (1998) is particularly important in this regard:

> While many factors contribute to differences in both the quality of life and premature death among Blacks in the United States, the role of *cultural mistrust* has often been overlooked. In an important early study of trust dispositions among Blacks and Whites, Terrell and Barrett (1979) found that Blacks, the poor and women were more likely to mistrust. The authors explained these empirical findings by referring to the psychology of oppressed groups whose social history does not support a belief system characterized as trusting. Consequently, politically disadvantaged groups who have experienced long-standing discrimination and prejudice tend to mistrust those identified with their oppressors (Terrell and Terrell, 1983). (p. 86)

He goes on to argue that a failure on the part of professionals to be sensitive to this low level of trust can easily produce a further layer of discrimination, what he calls 're-victimization'. Approaches to helping that take no account of racism and its consequences are therefore potentially counterproductive, if not actually oppressive in their own right.

Voice of experience 7.2

❝The misguided idea that we should promote equality by 'treating everybody the same' has led to a lot of black people not getting the support they need. It's bad enough when this happens at any time, but it is particularly worrying when it happens when people are grieving, when they are at their most vulnerable.**❞**

Carl, an equalities officer in a local authority

Clearly, then, there are various sets of vulnerability factors that we need to take into consideration if we are to develop an adequate understanding of how complicated grief can arise. When we combine these vulnerability factors with the significant issues connected with the nature of loss experience, as discussed above, we can see that there is considerable potential there for grieving to go awry, as it were, or for people to struggle even more than is usual with the challenges of grief. In such circumstances they may need professional help in coming to terms with the changes that have been forced upon them by the loss.

Unhelpful reactions to the loss

We have already noted the importance of social reactions in terms of stigma and disenfranchised grief, and how these can relate to issues of discrimination that are rooted in social attitudes (among other things). However, there are also personal responses to consider. Different people will, of course, respond to a loss situation in different ways. Often the way a person responds will be helpful and constructive, and will help them move forward in the healing process of grief. However, this is not always the case. Some people may behave in ways that are counterproductive, acting in such a way as to add to the difficulties of coping with the loss.

There is another parallel here with pressure and stress, in so far as it is not uncommon for people who are under considerable pressure to attempt to cope in ways which, although intended to make the situation better, have the effect of making them worse. For example, someone may attempt to cope with their pressures by drinking heavily, but that can then bring even more pressures as a result of the consequences of excessive alcohol consumption. We then have another vicious circle.

So, when we recognize that, in responding to grief, we are trying to cope with the pressures involved in a difficult situation, we also need to be aware that the same can happen when people are grieving. Consider the following examples

- At a *psychological* level, a grieving individual may become aggressive, and thereby alienate people and, in the process, cut off potential sources of support.

- At the *social* level, it may be that a grieving person cuts him- or herself off from his or her usual social connections. They can become so withdrawn that, once again, they deprive themselves of social support which, as noted earlier, has been recognized as a key factor in helping people with their grieving.
- There is also the *spiritual* dimension to this, in so far as people can respond to a loss in a way that makes their maintenance of any sense of spiritual path more difficult. For example, people can become bitter and resentful. They may lose their religious faith and then feel at a loss, and people who had no religious faith in the first place can lose their faith in humanity. They can therefore feel completely alienated as a result of their loss (especially if it is a traumatic loss).

The overall result, therefore, is that an individual's response to their loss may create a vicious circle in which their actions and reactions cut off potential sources of support, as well as potential sources of nourishment for the difficult journey they have now embarked upon. In this way, the loss can become characterized by complicated grief because what was already a difficult process has now become all the more difficult as a result of the destructive vicious circle that has developed.

The effects of complicated grief

What we have not looked at so far is why complicated grief is so important and why it is worthy of our attention. The answer to the question of why we should take it seriously is twofold. On the one hand, it is where there are complications in the grieving process that we are more likely to be involved as professional helpers. As noted earlier, the vast majority of people will manage their grief with nothing more than their usual inner personal resources and the social resources they can draw upon from their everyday networks of friends, family, colleagues and so on. It is generally where there are problems in relation to these helping factors that a professional may be called upon to be involved.

PRACTICE FOCUS 7.3

Olive was an education social worker who ran a support group for children who had lost a parent, brother or sister. She was a very experienced and knowledgeable worker. However, one day she attended a course on stress management and learned about how some people can make their pressures worse by behaving in what are, after all, counterproductive ways – for example, by denying that there is a problem and trying to press on with their lives regardless. What occurred to Olive was that she could see how this also applied to the children in her group. She recognized that there were very strong parallels, as she frequently encountered situations where the children were dealing with their grief in ways that were often unhelpful. On the course she commented that she could see how there were parallels between what the trainer was talking about and some of the reactions to grief she came across in her groupwork. The trainer was very interested to hear this and said that she could understand what Olive meant, as she saw grief as another set of pressures that we are called upon to deal with. Olive had read a lot of literature about grief, but she now realized that there was also much to be learned from learning about how people cope with pressure and stress.

The second reason for taking complicated grief so seriously is that, where it is not addressed effectively, it can result in two sets of other problems. The first set is *psychological* problems, and we shall look at these in more detail in Chapter 8. Complicated grief can also at times be a key factor in relation to *social* problems, and we shall explore these in Chapter 9.

For now, then, it is important to note that complicated grief is, as the name implies, a complicated matter, but it is also a very important one to which we need to pay a great deal of attention if we are to be well placed to rise to the professional challenges involved in helping people who are grieving – especially people who are having additional difficulties in relation to the loss or losses they have experienced.

Responding to complicated grief

When it comes to responding to complicated grief, we need to recognize that there are different levels of help. The first one is informal help or support – from friends, family, neighbours and so on. Professionals can do this too, just as human beings, but it is not necessarily part of the professional repertoire in itself; it is just what we do as human beings connecting with other human beings. Consequently, volunteers can also be important in this regard. They can be very helpful in offering this level of support when there is no-one else to do this, or where existing informal sources of support are quite limited (in situations where somebody has a low level of social capital, for example). The invaluable role and contribution of volunteers should not be underestimated.

Voice of experience 7.3

❝We have had occasional problems with volunteers who do not take to the work and soon move on, but most people do a great job and build up a lot of useful skills over time, skills that we find very useful.❞

Tricia, a volunteer coordinator at a hospice

The second level of help is what I would call professional non-specialist. This applies to the full range of helping professionals who, as part of their day-to-day jobs, can bear witness to grief and be helpful in the wide variety of ways that we have already discussed earlier in the book. This is where we are using our professional skills to help people who are in distress, just as we would try and help anyone else who is in distress for any other reasons that are not associated with grief. The third level, however, is professional specialist help. This is where the circumstances are so severe or worrying that it makes it necessary, or at least advisable, for somebody with specialist knowledge of tackling grief-related issues to be called upon to deal with these circumstances. Again, it is important to return to the point I emphasized in Chapter 6 that this may well be a counsellor or even a psychotherapist, but it does not have to be. There are various professionals who have developed high-level specialist skills when it comes to dealing with complex and complicated grief situations, not least: social workers; psychologists; psychiatrists; nurses (psychiatric and general); occupational therapists; family therapists; and so on.

Conclusion

As we have noted, it is important not to confuse complicated grief with pathological grief, this now largely discredited idea that some people grieve in an 'abnormal' way that is assumed to be indicative of some sort of mental disorder because it differs from the so-called 'normal' way of grieving. There are two things that we need to note in this regard. First of all, different people grieve in different ways. There is therefore a great diversity in terms of how people respond to their loss experiences. We have to make sure that we do not adopt a narrow focus on this and assume that, because somebody is grieving in a way that we do not regard as characteristic or as standardized in some way, we can therefore conclude that there is something wrong with them or wrong with how they are grieving. That is an unnecessarily judgemental approach that does not do justice to the need to value diversity.

Second, what is also important to note is that, even where the grieving patterns go beyond what can be regarded as the everyday diversity of grieving patterns, where the way somebody is grieving is creating, or is accompanied by, additional problems, it is still not helpful to think of this as a pathology, as something 'wrong' with the individual, some sort of metaphorical disease. While the term 'complicated' grief is not ideal, its great strength is that it emphasizes that what we are dealing with is a range of situations in which the generally constructive, if painful and exhausting, process of healing that we associate with grieving has additional factors that can lead to further challenges and difficulties. It further emphasizes that these additional challenges can, in turn, lead to a person's coping responses being overwhelmed. For this reason, it is important to connect the idea of complicated grieving with crisis and trauma, as discussed in Chapter 2 and with pressure and stress issues more broadly.

The overall message of this chapter, then, is that there are very many situations where the usually positive process of healing that we associate with grieving can go awry for a wide variety of reasons. It is often in these circumstances that professional help is called upon to supplement the informal help that would normally be available to individuals or families. Having reviewed the significance of complicated grief, what we are now going to do is begin the process of exploring the psychological and social problems that can arise as a result of complicated grief. To begin with, we will look at grief and psychological problems and this will form the subject matter of Chapter 8.

POINTS TO PONDER

- In your line of work (or the line of work you are studying for) what are the potential factors that could contribute to the development of complicated grief?
- Why is it important to distinguish carefully between 'ordinary' grief and complicated grief?
- How might you recognize that someone is experiencing complicated grief?

Key texts

1. Cox, G., Bendiksen, R. and Stevenson, R. (eds) (2002) *Complicated Grieving and Bereavement: Understanding and Treating People Experiencing Loss*, Amityville, NY, Baywood.
2. Goldman, L. (2002) *Breaking the Silence: A Guide to Helping Children with Complicated Grief – Suicide, Homicide, AIDS, Violence and Abuse*, New York, Routledge.
3. Neimeyer, R. A., Harris, D. L., Winokuer, H. R. and Thornton, G. F. (2011) *Grief and Bereavement in Contemporary Society*, New York, Routledge.

8

Grief and psychological problems

Introduction

In this chapter the emphasis is on how experiences of grief (especially unresolved and/or traumatic grief) can have profound and long-lasting effects on people's mental well-being. It can give rise to depression (short term and long), low self-esteem, neurotic disorders, addictions, aggression and violence, and even psychotic disorders. The main aim of this chapter, therefore, is to demonstrate that grief, if not handled well with adequate and appropriate support, can be extremely detrimental. By the same token, it shows that many of the psychological problems members of the helping profession encounter are likely to have their roots in loss and grief, especially where trauma is involved.

One important point to stress is that grief is not in itself a psychological problem. The theme throughout this book has been the importance of recognizing grief as a process of healing and, although it may involve extremes of pain and suffering at times, it is none the less a positive and constructive process that enables us to move from one phase of our life (prior to the loss) to the next. Grief, then, is not in itself a psychological problem, but the intense experiences associated with a loss can result in a wide range of psychological problems and this chapter will provide an overview of the main ones although, realistically, not all of them.

Stress, crisis and trauma

All three of these phenomena – stress, crisis and trauma – have the potential to lead to significant psychological problems. Let us look at each of these in turn so that we can develop a fuller understanding of their significance:

- *Stress.* As noted in Chapter 7, the pressures of everyday life can combine with the additional demands of having to cope with one or more losses to produce a level of pressure that strains our normal coping resources. This brings us back to the important distinction between pressure and stress that was also discussed in Chapter 7. Pressure is neutral, in the sense that it can be positive or negative. It can be positive in so far as it can motivate and even inspire people; it can be a great source of job satisfaction and pleasure. It can also be negative, in the sense that too much pressure (or even, sometimes, too little pressure) can lead to stress, can lead to the experience where the pressures are in some way harming our health, our well-being, our relationships or some other important aspects of our life. What can happen, then, is that the additional pressures associated with a loss experience can lead to a cumulative effect which then pushes our normal levels of pressure across the line to produce stress. That is, our day-to-day pressures overspill into stress when the further demands of grieving are added to our everyday pressures.

- *Crisis.* When those pressures become stress, they put strain on our normal coping resources. That strain can reach the point where our coping resources are overwhelmed; it takes us beyond the level at which we can cope. Then, as we saw in Chapter 2, we have a crisis situation, we experience a turning point where we cannot go on as we did before because our normal ways of coping are no longer adequate for the demands we are currently facing. This is not necessarily a problem for us, because a crisis, like pressures as described above, can be positive or negative. A crisis can be the basis of growth, development and new ways of coping, a process of empowerment. However, a crisis can also be debilitating and very harmful if not handled well – for example, if people do not receive the support they need when they need it. Consequently, where grief instigates a crisis, there is the potential for considerable harm to result.

- *Trauma.* As we noted in Chapter 2, stress arises when our normal coping methods are strained. A crisis occurs when our normal coping methods are overwhelmed. A trauma is where our normal coping methods are devastated, where it is not just a crisis in which a line has been crossed, so that we now have to find new ways of coping. A trauma can be so intensely powerful and destructive that it leaves us feeling totally at sea, with a sense that we may never cope again. In this way, it can be seen as an extreme form of crisis. However, the same rules apply in a sense. That is, while a trauma can be extremely painful, it leaves us in a situation where things may get better (what is known as post-traumatic growth, very similar to the transformational grief discussed earlier). But trauma can also lead to immense destruction, leaving the person so devastated by the experience they have undergone that they struggle to maintain any sense of normality in their life. This is sometimes medicalized in terms of 'post-traumatic stress disorder', but the reality is more complex than this. What we need is a more holistic understanding of such matters (Bracken, 2003; Thompson, 2009a).

Clearly, then, stress, crisis and trauma are all important issues that can be closely associated with people having psychological problems as a result of some form of grief reaction. They can be seen to apply where the additional pressures associated with grieving strain, overwhelm or even devastate our ability to cope with those pressures. Of course, this raises significant issues for professional helpers. We need to be aware of these processes and the dangers involved if we are to be in a strong enough position to offer effective help.

Identity

Identity is a good way of illustrating the holistic perspective that I have advocated earlier – that is, the biopsychosocial and spiritual

---

PRACTICE FOCUS 8.1

Francine was a school nurse who often provided care and support beyond the call of duty. She was particularly keen to be of help to children who were grieving. She was aware that she should not cross boundaries and try to be a professional counsellor, but she also knew that she could be of great help simply by listening and being someone who cared enough to give them the time and space to talk. However, she also knew when it was appropriate to refer the children on for more specialist help. Over the years she had come to recognize those children who had additional stresses and strains that meant they needed more help than just being listened to. She understood that grief was not in itself a psychological problem requiring specialist help, but also realized that sometimes specialist help was precisely what was needed, especially when there were other unresolved issues and sources of pressure that needed attention.

---

approach. There is a biological underpinning to who we are – for example, in terms of our body and other biological characteristics, the *fait accompli* that we are faced with in terms of our biological makeup. However, there is a strong tendency for people to overestimate the significance of biology and thereby underestimate the significance of other factors. It is therefore important to stress the other aspects of identity, the psychological aspects as well as the social aspects (who we are is largely a social issue as well as a personal one – Lawler, 2008; Parekh, 2008) and, of course, the spiritual, the sense of who we are and how we fit into the world (Moss, 2005).

Voice of experience 8.1

❝I am glad that spirituality is getting a lot of attention these days. I think it has been missed off the agenda for far too long. It is about time more people realized that we can't really help people if we have no sense of their spiritual needs, no sense of their 'take' on the world, and particularly their take on their world.**❞**

Val, a youth and community worker

A key part of identity is what is known as self-concept. This can be divided into three main parts:

- *Self-image*. This refers to how we perceive ourselves, what image we have of ourselves. It involves such questions as: who am I? And, in times of grief and loss, am I me any more? Can I be me without whom or what I have lost?
- *Self-esteem*. This is about self-worth, asking ourselves: am I a worthy person? Do I deserve good things in my life? Have I earned the right to be happy? It is therefore closely linked to the idea of confidence. So, at times of grief, self-esteem can be adversely affected. Confidence can go down; we can feel that we are no longer worthy. We can wonder whether we will ever be capable again, whether we will ever be able to move out of the debilitated state we find ourselves in now and re-establish some sense of normality and some degree of self-esteem.
- *Self-efficacy*. This refers to our ability to organize ourselves to cope in a reasonably disciplined way with the demands of everyday life, so that we are reasonably effective in going about our business. When we experience a loss, self-efficacy can be seriously undermined. We can become disorganized. We can lose our sense of routine or rhythm. This can lead to a sense of lack of control that can then produce a degree of stress (this is because a lack of control has been recognized as a key factor in the development of stress – Thompson, 2009d). Overall, then, self-efficacy can be quite problematic at times when we are wrestling with the difficulties of a significant loss.

This undermining of our sense of identity can have potentially very harmful effects. If we are no longer sure of who we are, that we are worthy of respect, for example, and that we are competent and capable, then we can develop a sense of helplessness and hopelessness. This can go a step further at times to become a nihilistic sense of 'nothing matters'. If we feel we have lost so much, then we begin to wonder whether it is worth caring about what is left. That can lead to destructive behaviour either outwardly towards other people in a sort of 'couldn't care less' attitude, or it can go inwards in terms of self-destructive behaviour. This can take the form of self-harm, self-

---

PRACTICE FOCUS 8.2

Eryl was a social worker who worked in the mental health field. She used various methods in her work, but relied heavily on cognitive behavioural therapy. She could see that it was very effective at bringing about short-term improvements. However, she could also see that, in many cases, the improvement was not sustained over time. After attending a course on promoting self-efficacy, she started using the lessons she had learned not only to improve her own self-efficacy, but also that of her clients. This proved to be very effective most of the time. However, what she soon came to learn was that, when she was working with people who were grieving, the improvements they had previously made in self-efficacy could easily be lost, in the short term at least. She realized that she would need to be tuned in to the impact of grief on people's ability to manage their everyday lives.

---

neglect (failing to eat properly, for example, or taking no notice of hygiene issues, and so on) or reckless behaviour (driving dangerously, for example, as if we have no concern about the consequences of having an accident).

What can also happen when this sense of identity is undermined is that, if we no longer value ourselves, we may be reluctant to form relationships. If we do not see ourselves as having anything worthwhile to offer other people, we may then cut ourselves out from potential sources of support by not wanting to form relationships. When this is added to the tendency to believe, after a relationship has ended (and we have experienced the painful grief associated with this), that we no longer want to take the risk of forming an attachment to someone else and thereby risk facing further grief if that attachment should be broken at any time in the future.

Voice of experience 8.2

❝I work with care leavers and help to prepare them for independence. Many of them have been abused and experienced an awful lot of losses, so they find it very difficult to trust anyone. I sometimes wonder how easy they will find it to partner up with someone when they find it so difficult to risk loving someone.❞

Marsha, a leaving care personal adviser

A further important factor in relation to identity is the need to recognize that we cannot do people's grieving for them – we can only support them in their grieving, accompany them on the journey, as it were. Attig (2011) makes an important point about this when he argues that:

> Caregivers should resist the temptation to do the difficult work of coping for us when we are bereaved. Our coping with loss is a personal experience, as is all coping. No other person can grieve for us. The challenges are ours to meet; the choices are ours to make. Yet, there is much that others can do for us as we relearn our worlds, find new places in our physical and social surroundings, learn how to continue to care about those who have died in their absence, and struggle to find new, meaningful, and hopeful directions for our life stories. (p. 23)

This passage eloquently explains that, in helping people cope with grief, we need to respect who they are, acknowledge *their* identity, *their* way of grieving and the new meanings that are contributing to developing *their* story. This seems obvious while calmly reading a book, but in the pressured situation of working with a grieving person, our anxieties can easily lead us into trying to impose our own solution, especially if we are feeling powerless and helpless and feel we would benefit from having a stronger degree of control over the situation.

Inward emotion

The point was made earlier that our emotional response to grief can be turned inwards. This can lead to some very strong feelings. For example, we can feel guilty even when, in an objective sense, we have nothing to feel guilty about. This can take the form of 'survivor guilt'. This refers to situations where someone has died or experienced some sort of other loss (for example, being made redundant or laid off) and we are left feeling guilty that it was not us. 'Why did he or she face this and not me?' can be an important question which can lead to an irrational sense of guilt. But, being irrational is nothing unusual in a grief reaction.

Anxiety can also feature strongly in grief-related situations. The sense of insecurity and vulnerability associated with grief can lead to high levels of anxiety, and where people are already prone to anxiety, this can be very significant. But, even where there is no background of anxiety-related problems, and there is just an everyday level of anxiety, the further anxiety brought about by a loss can be of significant proportions, potentially resulting in problems for the grieving individual and for those around him or her.

There is also depression to consider, as this can produce very serious psychological problems that can lead to a wide range of problems not only for the grieving person, but also for anyone connected with him or her. I have already emphasized the important point that we should not confuse grief, which is a positive process of healing, with depression, which is where our feelings are not going anywhere, where they have been numbed in a sense by the difficulties that we face. However, it is important to recognize that depression can arise as a result of grief, and so it is important that we are clear about the different manifestations of grief on the one hand and depression on the other, so that we do not (i) adopt a superficial approach where we confuse the two; or (ii) assume that what are actually signs of depression are simply signs of grief, and thereby fail to help somebody with their depression because we did not realize they were depressed.

Depression is particularly worrying where it does arise, as it has the tendency to produce a very negative mindset. It is as if the depressed person is wearing spectacles that block out anything positive, hopeful or enjoyable and only allows the wearer, to see the negative, the worrisome and the problematic aspects of their circumstances. This means that, once a person has become depressed, they are likely to find it very difficult to emerge from that depression, to adopt a more balanced and realistic approach to their life. This is problematic enough in general terms, but it is particularly concerning when it arises in situations involving loss and grief. This is because depression tends to have the effect of preventing the healing process of grief from taking place.

One further problem associated with depression is that the dominant approach to this psychosocial and spiritual phenomenon is a medicalized one – that is, one that is rooted in the biological aspect of humanity. It therefore has a tendency to neglect the other aspects of a person's life, thereby producing a distorted, reductionist understanding. If a grieving person becomes depressed and is subsequently led to believe that they are 'ill' or suffering from a 'mental illness', this can then lead them to look for a 'cure' to their condition, rather than try to understand – and seek support in dealing with – the psychological, social and spiritual challenges their loss has presented them with (again, the work of Schneider, 2000 and 2006, is very relevant and helpful in casting light on these issues).

What can be particularly problematic in terms of emotion that is directed inwards is when the combination of guilt, anxiety and depression lead to a form of emotional paralysis where people just do not feel able to move forward in any positive or constructive way. When this unfortunate and dangerous combination arises, the positive process of healing can be severely hampered and we can therefore encounter a situation of complicated grief as discussed in Chapter 7.

In terms of inward emotion, there can also be a significant sense of emptiness or void associated with the loss. In itself, this is quite normal and usual and nothing to be worried about. However, what can be a cause for concern is when some people attempt to fill that existential void in inappropriate ways. This can be through, for example, eating disorders (bulimia can be seen as a need to fill that void through overeating while anorexia can be seen as a way of trying to address that void by not eating, by in a sense being taken over by a sense of emptiness). There can also be drink problems. Excessive drinking can be part of an underlying drive to try and fill the emptiness that we associate so strongly and so powerfully with loss. Thirdly, the same argument can be applied to drug misuse. The emphasis on consuming, on filling can be closely related to our need to address the void that we are finding so difficult to cope with.

Overall, then, there are various ways in which our reaction to grief can be problematic in some respects as a result of how we deal

---

> **PRACTICE FOCUS 8.3**
>
> Tara was a nurse therapist who had just taken up her new post in a multidisciplinary trauma centre in a psychiatric hospital. When she did her professional training she had learned about psychodynamic perspectives but she did not pay much attention to them as she found the whole Freudian thing a bit far fetched. She preferred what she saw as more concrete methods and was particularly interested in solution-focused therapies. However, as she settled into her new job and spent a lot of time working with people who were struggling to cope with their grieving, she started to realize that so much of what she was seeing fitted well with the psychodynamic perspective, with its emphasis on oral fixation. She began to wonder whether she had been too dismissive of psychoanalytical ideas.

with emotions that are directed inwards. We clearly need to take such matters seriously and not lose sight of how much harm such emotional processes can do, not only to the person experiencing those emotions, but also their family, friends, colleagues and so on. If we are to be effective in helping people deal with their grief challenges, then we will need to have at least a basic understanding of what is involved and, ideally, build up that knowledge to a more advanced level over time.

While emotions that are directed inwards are important factors to take into consideration, they also need to be balanced by an understanding of how emotions directed outwards can also prove potentially problematic. It is therefore to this topic that we now turn.

Outward emotion

Experiences of loss generally generate high levels of emotion. As we have seen, much of this will be directed inwards, but there will also be the outward, more objective expressions of emotion to consider. These can take various forms and can be at varying levels of intensity and duration.

In terms of problematic reactions, the most common emotion is anger. People can feel angry and even bitter about the experiences they have had, and that anger can sometimes be expressed directly and openly where someone talks about why they feel angry about what has happened. However, that anger can also be addressed in not such an open way, in not such a self-aware way – for example, in the form of aggression. Someone can, in a sense, take out their anger inappropriately on others by being aggressive towards them. This can be verbal aggression or, in some circumstances, can even amount to physical aggression or violence. Thankfully this is not an everyday occurrence for most people, but nor is it particularly unusual. It happens quite frequently in a number of situations, and so it is not something that we can dismiss as a highly unlikely occurrence. We have to be tuned into the possibility of that happening and think carefully about how we handle that situation without responding to aggression either defensively or trying to fight fire with fire by returning the aggression. Either of those strategies is likely to prove counterproductive and potentially disastrous, as they could lead to the development of a vicious circle of constantly rising tensions.

It is important to acknowledge that, by associating anger with potential problems, I am not trying in any way to say that anger is not a legitimate response, or in any way to pathologize people who become angry in the face of a significant loss (indeed, the expression of anger that does not result in aggression or a backlash from other people can be very therapeutic and a helpful way of dealing with our feelings). Rather, I am arguing that anger presents an additional set of risks, an additional array of issues to consider when weighing up situations and judging how best to respond.

A further set of emotional responses that can be expressed outwardly is that of impatience. A grieving person can feel very tense, and that tension can then manifest itself as impatience. This can mean that it can be very difficult to help somebody who is grieving who begins to express their grief through impatience. So, for example, when you are trying to talk to somebody in a helpful way to perhaps guide them to engage in problem-solving activities, then that can be very, very difficult if they do not have the patience to listen to what you are trying to say and constantly cut across you with a terse, abrupt or even rude remark in response. But, in such circumstances, it is important that again we do not attempt to fight fire with fire by becoming impatient in return. In fact, the more impatient the person we are trying to help is, the more patient we need to be to counterbalance that.

Finally, in terms of outward emotional responses we have the problem of cynicism. The term 'cynicism' comes from the Greek word for dog κυνικωσ (kunikos), and so a cynic is somebody who behaves like dogs often do, in the sense of being someone who just curls up and minds their own business and takes no interest in wider issues, has no sense of commitment to anything else, just disconnects in this negative way from things that are going on around them. That analogy is an important one in general, but it is particularly important in terms of grief. I mentioned earlier in relation to identity that people can get to the point where they feel that nothing matters, that they have a sense that there is nothing further they can lose. This can also lead to a sense of cynicism, whereby they just simply do not care. They reach the point where they pay no attention to other things going on around them. So, for example, there can be problems here if a grieving parent becomes cynical and therefore uncaring towards their child or children. That in itself will clearly create further problems, an example of the vicious circle I mentioned earlier that can arise in terms of how we respond to grief – ways in which our response can actually make the situation worse and generate further problems, thereby potentially creating a very destructive, and hence 'vicious', circle.

This can be particularly significant in situations involving non-death-related losses. This is because other people may see the cynicism without seeing it as a possible grief reaction because, in the absence of a death, they do not see the situation as one that is rooted in loss and grief. This is another reason why it is so very important that we are tuned in to loss and grief in all their manifestations, and not simply when they arise in response to a bereavement.

What we have to realize is that any one of these outward expressions of emotion or any combination of anger, aggression, impatience or cynicism can have the effect of cutting off a grieving person from the support they need at perhaps the time they need it the most. So, when it comes to recognizing psychological problems associated with grief and being as well equipped as we can to help to deal with these, we clearly need to be aware of how grief can produce the outward expression of emotions in ways that are potentially very problematic and counterproductive, thereby possibly contributing to what in Chapter 7 I referred to as complicated grieving.

Voice of experience 8.3

❝What I try and impress upon our staff is the need to recognize that a lot of the children's behaviour is a reflection of the many losses they have experienced. Once staff appreciate that it is not simply a matter of being 'naughty' or of so-called challenging behaviour, they are more likely to be more understanding and supportive.❞

Jim, the manager of a children's home

Conclusion

I emphasized at the beginning of this chapter that we should not see grief as a psychological problem in itself. I would now want to add to that by saying that we should not see psychological problems as some sort of pathology, to see them as a manifestation of some sort of failing in an individual. Everybody at some point in their life will experience some kind of psychological problem, whether it is relatively minor in terms of, for example, a temporary loss of confidence and self-esteem, or relatively major in the form of some kind of severe emotional crisis or traumatic experience in our life. Our aim, then, is not to pathologize people who are experiencing grief-related psychological difficulties, but rather to paint a picture of the complexities involved and to provide a foundation of understanding, so that, as professional helpers, we are better equipped to help them to deal with their challenges, and indeed, to respond to the challenges we ourselves face as professional helpers, whether those challenges are at a personal level, as discussed in Chapter 5, or at a professional level, as discussed in Chapter 6.

We also need to recognize that the psychological problems associated with some forms of grief can add an extra layer of vulnerability. It is therefore important that we ensure that our practice is built on not only our professional knowledge base and the associated skills base, but also our professional value base. As Smith and Smith (2008) comment:

> people may seek us out when they are feeling vulnerable, and because of this there is a responsibility for us to act with integrity when meeting with the feelings and emotions of another. To have integrity means to act in a way that adheres to moral principles, for example, honesty. We have to handle people's emotions with sensitivity and care, and choose to act with good intention. (p. 50)

Of course, all our professional practice should be based on integrity, but when we are working with people who are probably at their lowest ebb, at their most vulnerable, then the need for integrity becomes even stronger.

As we have seen, possible psychological problems associated with grief are many and varied. We have noted, for example, that there is a wide range of potential problems associated with stress, crisis and trauma. There is also the undermining of identity (which has psychological, social and spiritual dimensions), as well as the expression of emotion inwardly that can result in emotional paralysis and other related difficulties, or the outward expression of emotion that can bring a wide range of problems, not least the separation from potential sources of support when we perhaps need them most. Clearly, then, we need to be tuned into these various potential or actual problems, so that we are better equipped to prevent them where possible, and to respond confidently and competently in whatever reasonable ways we can when they do arise.

POINTS TO PONDER

- How might your identity, your sense of who you are, influence how you grieve when faced with a significant loss?
- How might you recognize that someone's emotions that are being directed inwards are leading to psychological problems?
- How could you ensure that, in encountering anger on the part of a grieving person, you remain calm and do not add to the tension of the situation?

Key texts

1. Harvey, J. H. (2002) *Perspectives on Loss and Trauma: Assaults on the Self*, London, Sage.
2. Lawler, S. (2008) *Identity: Sociological Perspectives*, Cambridge, Polity.
3. Oatley, K., Keltner, D. and Jenkins, J. M. (2006) *Understanding Emotions*, London, John Wiley & Son.

9

Grief and social problems

Introduction

This chapter parallels the previous one, in so far as it explores problems connected with loss and grief, but here the emphasis is on the impact of grief in terms of *social* problems, rather than simply *psychological* ones. This includes crime, abuse (of children and vulnerable adults), social alienation and disaffection, violence, educational failure, family breakdown and homelessness. It makes the vitally important point that grief is a far more significant factor in human experience than generally tends to be recognized. As the final chapter, it is premised on the argument that the helping professions in particular and society in general need to pay much fuller attention to grief as a wide-ranging psychosocial and spiritual phenomenon, a fundamental aspect of the human condition, rather than a marginal, largely psychological matter that arises only when someone dies.

I begin by clarifying what I mean by social problems and why I feel it is important to draw links between them and grief. I then move on to consider a total of seven social problems and comment on how grief can be associated with each of them. Finally I illustrate the interconnections across social problems and consider how grief – especially traumatic grief – can be a linking thread.

Social problems: a psychosocial approach

Before considering the significance of grief in relation to social problems, it is worth pausing to consider what exactly we mean by

a social problem, and how we can best understand their significance.

A social problem can be defined as a problem that arises in relation to society itself:

> There is an important distinction to be drawn between social and
> personal problems, although the two often overlap. A social prob-
> lem is something that has an effect on society overall, or at least
> on certain sectors of society and indeed the social order. Often
> what is defined as a social problem is a problem which may well
> have significant implications for particular individuals, but is seen
> as particularly significant because of its implications for society
> itself (where, for example, the persistence of that problem may
> present a threat to society). (N. Thompson and S. Thompson,
> 2008, pp. 77–8)

It is not therefore simply the accumulation of personal problems
within a society, but rather something which proves problematic for
a society as an entity. Poverty would be a good example. It has a
detrimental effect not only on those people who are directly affected
by it, but also on wider society. While some would argue from a
broadly marxist perspective that poverty is a necessary feature of
capitalist society (the rich are rich because the poor are poor), it can
be argued that the prevalence of poverty is problematic for wider
society, largely, but not exclusively, because of its denial and undermining of citizenship and is therefore rightly a major concern of
social policy (Lister, 2004).

One important point we need to take on board is that social problems arise from an interplay (a dialectic, to use the technical term)
between individual actions and wider social patterns and institutions, in the sense that individual actions will contribute to the
broader phenomenon of a social problem (in the same way that individual criminal acts will contribute to crime as a whole), and that
problem will then have an impact on individual members of society
(direct and indirect victims of crime, people who have to pay higher
insurance premiums because of crime, law enforcement officers

---

> ### PRACTICE FOCUS 9.1
>
> Narcis was a community development worker with a particular interest in welfare rights and the development of anti-poverty strategies. In her work she had seen how devastating the effects of poverty could be on individuals and families, and she was particularly concerned with its impact on children as they were growing up in very difficult circumstances. However, what also struck her was the damage that poverty did to society as a whole. She could see clearly from her experience how poverty contributed to crime, violence, alcohol and drug problems, homelessness and social disaffection more broadly. She could also see that poverty meant many losses for so many of the people caught in its trap. It was for these reasons that she was so committed to using her role as a means of helping to tackle poverty and its consequences.

who are faced with additional work and so on) – see Clarke (2001) for an interesting discussion of the social roots of social problems.

A social problem is qualitatively different from a personal problem. For example, it is important to realize that crime is not simply the adding up of actual incidences of criminal behaviour, treated in isolation. This is because crime is not just a phenomenon characterized by a range of events that have an effect on the individual victims of criminal acts. It also has a significant impact on society as a whole. By seeing social problems in this way, we can see that there is a two-way relationship between individual behaviours and the social context in which those behaviours take place (Thompson, 2010).

Bracher (2009) offers an interesting perspective on social problems. He adopts what I have referred to earlier as a psychosocial approach – that is, one that draws on both psychological and sociological understandings. His particular emphasis is on identity and how behaviours that contribute to social problems can be linked to the maintenance and protection of identity. Given that losses (especially traumatic losses) can seriously destabilize our sense of self, temporarily at least, then Bracher's approach invites us to consider the significance of loss and grief to the development and maintenance of social problems.

It would be a serious mistake to assume that social problems are simply wider manifestations of psychological phenomena. This would be an example of reductionism, one of the four 'deadly sins' of theory development discussed by Sibeon (2004). It is therefore good to note that Bracher takes account of sociological factors, but he argues that we also have to take account of psychological factors, especially those of identity (which is, of course, also a sociological phenomenon – Lawler, 2008). Bracher argues that:

> research in multiple disciplines clearly demonstrates that the key factors in the construction of character and personality are to be found in the material, social, and cultural environments. The literature of sociology is replete with such explanations. However, most of these accounts fail to specify the nature of the causal (psychological) links between environment and behaviour. The present analysis, in contrast, reveals identity needs and vulnerabilities as the key causal links between environment and behaviour, explaining how various social and cultural factors damage (traumatize) identity and thus render it unable to maintain itself by more benign means. (2009, pp. xii–xiii)

The aim, then, is not to replace sociological explanations with psychological ones, but rather to integrate the two perspectives, to produce a genuinely psychosocial approach. Bracher goes on to argue that:

> Effective solutions to social problems must address the social and cultural environments in ways that *affect the identities* of the individuals engaging in the socially problematic behaviours. (p. xiii)

Voice of experience 9.1

❝One of the things I have learned from my experience here is that much of the criminal and anti-social behaviour we come across is partly down to adolescent boys trying to prove themselves, trying to prop up their fragile sense of self by doing daring things that they think their peers will approve of.**❞**

Jan, a youth justice worker

We noted in Chapter 7 that, in certain circumstances, grief can be 'complicated' – that is, the process of healing involved in grieving can be accompanied or even blocked by a range of problematic complications. These can affect people's behaviour in two ways:

(i) The grieving individual can behave in a range of ways that cause tensions and difficulties and which may be destructive or even self-destructive; and

(ii) The pressures and strains of living, or working, with someone who is struggling with complicated grieving can be of significant proportions and can lead to relationship breakdown or at least a very stressful relationship.

Such problematic behaviour and interactions can contribute to socially damaging consequences (drug misuse, violence, crime and so on). They can also reflect what I shall refer to as 'identity challenges' – that is, circumstances in which difficulties in maintaining our sense of self are encountered. In this way, we can begin to forge a perspective that is not only psychosocial, but also spiritual in so far as it encompasses important issues relating to who we are and how we see ourselves fitting into the wider world.

So, having clarified what we mean by social problems and begun to draw some links between social problems and grief, let us now explore some specific examples of how grief – especially complicated grief – can make a significant contribution to a wide range of social problems.

Crime and imprisonment

We have seen from research studies that grief is something that is closely associated with crime and particularly in relation to imprisonment. For example, Leach, Burgess and Holmwood (2008) inform us that:

A variety of studies have demonstrated that many prisoners have suffered from losses and trauma throughout their lives, and in many instances they have never received any support or interventions to address resultant problems. (p. 104)

There is also the issue of imprisonment itself, especially where the fact of imprisoning somebody can lead to further grief reactions – for example, for the children and other loved ones of the person who is in prison. Hames and Pedreira (2003) describe the children of imprisoned parents as disenfranchised grievers who are facing compounded losses. This is a telling comment, as it raises important issues about how children can become victims of a form of secondary punishment, facing potentially very significant stress and distress as a result of a parent being sent to prison. A study by Bocknek, Sanderson and Britner (2009) revealed a high prevalence of post-traumatic stress in children whose father had been imprisoned.

While it would be simplistic to argue that grief experiences simply 'cause' crime, it would also be a mistake not to recognize significant linkages between the two. It is perhaps no coincidence that the higher levels of grief experience among prisoners should arise in this way. We can see that, when somebody is experiencing complicated grief and is expressing their feelings outwardly and inappropriately through aggression or recklessness or by disregarding other people (as discussed in Chapter 7), this will then contribute to a wide variety of crimes. The sense of 'I couldn't care less' is one that can be closely associated with powerful experiences of grief.

Abuse

This is another area where we can see important linkages. This applies to three different types of abuse: child abuse, the abuse of vulnerable adults and domestic abuse (domestic violence). Let us consider each of these in turn:

- *Child abuse.* We are now aware that child abuse can have significant problematic effects, as mentioned earlier, and we are also aware that this can often lead to the abused becoming an abuser (Rymaszewska and Philpot, 2006). In this way we can see that much of today's problem of child abuse owes a great deal to the abuse that has taken place in earlier generations, and we are now seeing the effects of that abuse in the abusive behaviour of certain perpetrators (although it is important not to oversimplify this matter and assume that (i) all perpetrators were themselves abused as children, or (ii) being abused will necessarily turn somebody into a future abuser).

- *Abuse of vulnerable adults.* This has become a technical term, now used to refer to situations in which somebody, who is in a position where they find it difficult to protect themselves from exploitation and abuse, is mistreated by unscrupulous others. This would include people with limited mental capacity as a result of mental health problems, learning disabilities, dementia and related matters. It also incorporates people who are in a limited position to protect themselves due to physical difficulties, such as disability of various kinds. We can speculate that much of the abuse that occurs is as a result of unresolved grief issues. For example, as a practising social worker I encountered many situations where that was clearly the case.

- *Domestic violence.* We shall see below that family breakdown is often as a result of members of a family adopting different and incompatible styles of grieving and having insufficient tolerance of each other's approach to the challenges involved. This argument can then be extended to domestic violence. We can see that there are ways in which unresolved issues of grief (and especially trauma) can produce situations where the tensions in a family get so high that the result is one of violence. This is not to say that this is the only cause of domestic violence, as that would be a gross oversimplification of a complex issue, but it is reasonable to argue that it should be considered as one important contributory factor among many.

There are therefore clear links between abuse and grief that we can draw, although there is an element of speculation in some of these linkages. None the less, what should be quite clear is that there is enough concern about significant linkages to teach us that we need to look much more closely at this topic and build up our professional knowledge base.

PRACTICE FOCUS 9.2

Gwen and Steve were foster carers recruited by a specialist agency dedicated to working with children who had been traumatized by experiences of sexual abuse. Their basic training had helped them to understand that traumatized children would have grief issues to contend with, as psychological trauma involves a number of significant losses. When they had their first child to look after they could not see any signs of grief at first. However, after a while they began to see the aspects of grief they had been trained to recognize. It made them feel so sad to see a child so badly affected by what they had always thought of as an adult concern – coming to terms with a major loss, or set of losses. They knew that they would have to be on their mettle to help this little girl who seemed to have the weight of the world on her shoulders because of the abuse she had suffered at such a young age.

Social alienation and disaffection

Given what we know about how grief (particularly forms of complicated grief) can lead people to conclude that nothing matters and that they do not care about anything any more, it is understandable that much of the social alienation and disaffection that we witness in society can be linked to these experiences. One clear example of this would be the phenomenon of Hell's Angels, motorcycle users who have become notorious for causing trouble in various ways. They continue to exist to this day but in their heyday, when much was written about them (H. S. Thompson, 2003), it was noted that a high proportion of people who self-described themselves as Hell's Angels were veterans of war, particularly the Vietnam War. We can therefore begin to see connections between the trauma associated with war and the sense of recklessness and 'couldn't care less' attitude that is characteristic of the behaviour and, indeed, culture of the Hell's Angels phenomenon.

Arguably, this is just one example of a much wider phenomenon of people feeling estranged from wider society because of issues of grief – especially traumatic grief – that they are wrestling with. For example, Thomas and Bracken (2008) make some challenging comments about the neglect of loss (and related factors) in the field of mental health:

> The single most harmful aspect of modern psychiatry is its failure to face up to and engage with personal suffering, stories of tragedy, loss, abuse and oppression. The biological reductionism that now dominates has served to marginalize approaches that foreground these issues. This in our view is a deep moral and spiritual failing that can only be rectified by a major overhaul of the epistemology of psychiatry, and the way that doctors are trained. (p. 49)

Nicholls (2007) also has some important points to make about this subject. While it is not simply a matter of arguing that loss 'causes' mental health problems, there is clearly an important field of study that has received relatively little attention. The emphasis on loss and suffering in relation to mental well-being is clearly consistent with the growing emphasis on spirituality in the helping professions (Moss, 2005).

Voice of experience 9.2

❝We did an exercise on a training course about loss and grief that helped us to understand why children who have experienced so many losses end up lashing out because they feel they have nothing to lose and have so much pent-up frustration inside them. It made me realize too that it is not just children that it can happen to.**❞**

Andrew, a psychiatric nurse

Violence

A well-documented phenomenon is that of the cycle of violence (Parkes, 2008). This refers to the way in which certain instances of violence can then produce further instances (in retaliation, for example) but can also produce a culture in which violence becomes accepted as the norm. Given the links drawn above between grief and crime, grief and abuse, grief and alienation and disaffection, then it takes only a small leap of logic to speculate that grief issues may be at the root of much of the violence that is a feature of our society today.

One very telling example of this would be terrorism. There is a persuasive argument that the war on terror that has emerged in the media and popular culture, primarily as a response to the 9/11 atrocities in 2001, has significant linkages with grief and trauma:

> Warren [2006] develops an interesting analysis of terrorism and the war on terror in terms of they can both be seen as a reaction to the trauma brought about by earlier conflicts and atrocities. There is a danger, then, that not only will terrorism cause trauma, but also further atrocities will be the result of traumatic reactions that call for blood. There is a danger, then, of a vicious circle developing. (Thompson, 2009a, p. 64)

Violence is often a reaction to feelings of being humiliated or disrespected, when people feel that they have lost face or have been treated in a dishonourable way (Baumeister, 2001). We can begin to see links between this and the way people often respond to a loss. Where somebody experiences a trauma, for example, they can feel devastated by that experience, and that can lead to a sense of shame and humiliation and also anger, particularly if there is somebody or something that can be blamed for the trauma (such as terrorism on a societal scale or a perpetrator of abuse on a personal scale).

Educational failures

It is important to emphasize that I am using the word failure to refer to failures in the system, rather than to individual difficulties in terms of educational achievement – my aim is not to pathologize children who struggle within the school system. While educational difficulties for individuals can be significant problems, they are personal problems and therefore more in the territory of Chapter 8 than the social problems I am trying to concentrate on here. My argument is that society as a whole loses out through failures in our educational processes to produce better results in terms of overall educational outcomes for people. The work of Rowling (2003) shows that grief is an important factor in school life and often one that is not well addressed. It is therefore relatively easy to surmise that some educational problems at least will have their roots in loss and grief issues, partly as a result of not being given the attention they deserve within the education system. Stevenson (2000) and others have made similar points to emphasize the significant nature of the failure to address loss and grief issues in educational settings.

Family breakdown

There are various reasons why family breakdown can occur and I shall be arguing here that a key one among them is difficulties in terms of members of a family having conflicting ways of dealing with loss situations. Here it is important to emphasize that family breakdown, as well as being clearly a problem for members of the family concerned, is also a social problem, in so far as a high rate of family breakdown has significant implications for the wider operation of society.

Riches and Dawson (2000) undertook an important research study in which they interviewed parents who had lost a son or daughter. One of the key findings from this study was that the divorce and separation rate for people involved in the study was significantly higher than the national average. As a result of their investigations, the authors came to the conclusion that a key factor here was that parents often adopted conflicting styles of grieving and found it difficult to accommodate their partner's style of grieving. These additional tensions seem to be, in many cases, sufficient to lead to the couple separating. I have also, in my own professional experience, encountered this situation many times. There is, then, clearly an important set of links between family breakdown and how loss issues are dealt with in families.

Linked to this is the question of divorce itself producing a range of losses and therefore potentially setting up a vicious circle. Kroll (2002) provides a useful overview of the loss issues involved in divorce. She makes the important observation that:

> Divorce and parental separation are facts of life ... Everyone in the family will be affected, but the most vulnerable and power-less are the children. Understanding their experiences of loss and grief, managing their powerful feelings and enabling them to achieve either resolution or a way of being that enables them to cope are important tasks; at a time of significant need, they deserve an equal service. (pp. 123–4)

In addition, Baum (2003) alerts us to the fact that there are significant gender differences in terms of the impact of divorce and how people deal with its aftermath.

PRACTICE FOCUS 9.3

Caitlin was a Relate counsellor with many years' experience in the marriage guidance and relationship counselling field. She had realized that divorce or separation involves a wide range of losses, and she was also aware that men and women often responded very differently both to separation and to the losses associated with it. However, it was only when her own brother went through a divorce that it fully hit home to her how different his response was to what her own would have been in those circumstances. He became uncharacteristically angry and aggressive. The situation put her in a difficult position because she wanted to help and support him as a loving sister, but she knew it would be hard for her to maintain her professional boundaries by not trying to counsel him. She realized that this was going to be quite a challenging situation to help her brother deal with the losses he was experiencing.

Homelessness

Partly as a combination of some of the factors outlined above, many people can find that they are in a situation where they no longer have security of tenure for their accommodation. This can refer to situations in which people are literally 'on the streets', but can also apply to people who are homeless, in the sense that they have no current abode that they have a direct right to occupy. Homelessness can contribute to other social problems, such as crime, drug abuse and so on, but is also a significant problem in its own right. It is therefore worth considering how loss can lead to situations of homelessness. Consider the following examples, each of which I have encountered in my professional life:

- A 16-year old girl informed her deeply religious parents that she was pregnant and they refused to have her in the house as they were so deeply ashamed. The parents tried to arrange for her to stay with her older, married sister, but she refused to go and ended up homeless, having to rely on the hospitality of her friends on a short-term basis and very fearful of what would happen on a longer-term basis.
- A 43-year-old man had been living with his partner for over five years in her privately rented flat. When she died he became quite depressed. He had no legal right to stay in the flat, as it had been registered in her name a few years before he moved in with her and they had never taken the trouble to change it to a joint tenancy. His landlord could have offered him the ongoing tenancy, but felt that it would be too risky to have a tenant that he perceived to be 'mentally ill'. He therefore issued a 'notice to quit', thereby adding one more name to the list of homeless people in that area.
- A 20-year-old university student 'hit the bottle' when both his parents were killed in a car crash. The university authorities were unaware of the circumstances, and so when his drinking became out of control, they asked him to leave his course and vacate his room at the hall of residence.
- A 23-year-old woman had a miscarriage and was so devastated by the losses involved that she left her husband in their rural home and went to London, even though she had nowhere to stay there and little money to pay for accommodation. Her

husband had no idea why she had behaved in such an uncharacteristic way, and she herself seemed to have little more understanding of her own behaviour.

- A 49-year-old man was devastated when his business went bankrupt. He became very withdrawn much of the time and operated on a short fuse a great deal of the rest of the time, leading to the departure of his wife who could no longer cope with his mood swings. Partly as a result of the bankruptcy and partly as a consequence of his inability to cope with the cumulative losses of his business and livelihood, that is, the loss of his self-esteem and self-respect; his role as provider; and, perhaps most significantly of all, his much-loved wife, he failed to pay the mortgage for several months and was subsequently made homeless when the property was repossessed.

- A 15-year-old girl was sexually abused by her stepfather. Out of shame she could not face telling her mother about what had happened, and so she left home. She became involved in the drug scene and was at risk of becoming involved in prostitution.

As these examples illustrate, grief can be a key factor contributing to behaviours which, while problematic for the individuals concerned, are also problematic at a societal level, as they reinforce the social problem of homelessness which can lead to many other social problems. Indeed, the interconnections across social problem areas is such an important issue that it merits a fuller discussion, and so it is to these that we now turn.

Interconnections

For the sake of clarity in making the points I have wanted to put forward in this chapter I have examined the various social problems in isolation from one another. However, in reality, social problems do not operate in isolation; they interact and reinforce one another, often producing vicious circles. When we include grief in the mix, we can see that there is considerable scope for such vicious circles to do a great deal of harm. The following possibilities illustrate this:

- Family breakdowns can lead to homelessness, bringing about losses related to both the family breakdown itself and the subsequent homelessness. These additional losses and the pressures they bring can then make the likelihood of family reconciliation much more remote.

- Homelessness is often a key factor in drug abuse. It is often when people are 'on the streets' or otherwise without somewhere they can call home that they can be (i) vulnerable to the appeal of the escapism offered by drugs; and (ii) more likely to come into contact with drug dealers. Of course, it can also work the other way round: drug addiction can lead to someone being made homeless.

- Drug abuse is one of the most common reasons for criminal behaviour, illustrating a further way in which one social problem can exacerbate another. Where people have become reliant on drugs, then the burning desire to get the next 'fix' will often lead to crimes being committed to secure the funds to pay for drugs.

- Crime, of course, often leads to imprisonment, and, as we have already noted in this chapter, that can bring significant problems for family members left behind, especially for children. One such problem is a higher risk of poverty and deprivation – concerns which, in turn, are likely to feature among the list of factors that contribute to criminal behaviour.

- Poverty and deprivation can be seen as major causes of social alienation and disaffection, especially when we understand poverty in relative terms – that is, a matter of being excluded from social norms (Lister, 2004). Poverty and deprivation are also associated with poor housing, crime, drug abuse and thus are key factors in relation to social alienation and disaffection.

- Social alienation and disaffection can then be understood as important factors in the development of violence. Where there is less of a sense of belonging and community spirit, it is understandable that there will be a greater propensity towards violence. Such violence can range from minor to major in scale and impact.

- Violence can manifest itself as abuse. This could be child abuse (Corby, 2005) or the abuse of vulnerable adults (Martin, 2007), but can also include domestic violence in which women (and sometimes men) are subject to assaults at the hands of their partner (Amiel and Heath, 2003). While not all abuse involves direct violence in a physical sense, abuse can none the less be said to do violence to the recipients of its malice.
- Abuse, especially child abuse, can be a significant contributory factor in relation to educational failure, and all forms of abuse can contribute to family breakdown, taking us back to the beginning.

Of course, these are not the only interconnections that can be drawn, but this overview should provide a sufficiently clear picture of how important it is to try to understand social problems holistically, rather than in isolation. Based on the ideas presented in this chapter we should also be able to see how loss and grief can be recognized as significant aspects of how people's actions and interactions can contribute to the development and maintenance of social problems.

Voice of experience 9.3

❝In my job I see so many problems – personal problems, family problems, community problems, and so often they are all intertwined. I try to do my bit as a nurse but I meet so many people who need help for so many different problems. It really shows how important it is for professionals to work together.**❞**

Anji, a community nurse

Conclusion

As I emphasized earlier, a social problem is not just a problem for the individuals or families concerned. It is something that has wider implications for society as a whole or at least for significant sectors of society. In this brief overview of a range of social problems in which I have drawn linkages with grief (and sometimes especially traumatic grief), we have begun to see how complex this scenario is. What makes it even more complex is that these social problems (and the various other ones that space has not allowed me to explore in this chapter) will interact and potentially make each other worse. What we tend to face, then, is a very intricate web of destructive forces within society, many of which are fuelled by issues of loss and grief. What this means is that we need to move away from the idea that grief is primarily a personal problem and mainly a psychological matter and recognize that there are significant social aspects to grief, in so far as unresolved grief issues can be major factors in the development and maintenance of social problems.

What we also need to recognize is that, in some circumstances, our responses to social problems can cause further problems. For example, linking back to a scenario I described earlier, when somebody is imprisoned as a result of crimes (which may themselves have their roots in grief issues), this can have a significant knock-on effect for key people within their network, especially in the case of parents or their children. There is therefore much for us to consider in terms of developing our knowledge and understanding of the complexities of grief as a holistic phenomenon involving biological, psychological, sociological and spiritual issues. In effect, what we have to acknowledge is that grief is a complex and multi-faceted phenomenon that has wide application across a range of situations and is not just a psychological issue restricted to a narrow range of events or phenomena.

POINTS TO PONDER

- How might grief contribute to crime?
- What loss issues are involved in homelessness?
- How might the interconnections across social problems have an impact on the work you do (or that you are training to do)?

Key texts

1. Baumeister, R. F. (2001) *Evil: Inside Human Violence and Cruelty*, New York, Henry Holt and Co.
2. Bracher, M. (2009) *Social Symptoms of Identity Needs: Why We Have Failed to Solve Our Social Problems and What to Do About It*, London, Karnac.
3. Bracken, P. (2003) *Trauma: Culture, Meaning and Philosophy*, London, Whurr.

Conclusion

We have travelled a long way in just nine short chapters, covering an extensive terrain and engaging with some very complex and subtle issues. Of course, that is still just the tip of the iceberg, and so I must reiterate the point I made in the Introduction that this book will not provide you with all that you need to know. It is in many ways a 'gateway' text, one that should present many new pathways of learning and encourage you to pursue at least some of them, with the 'Guide to further learning' as one way of planning your future studies and learning.

However, the book should have given you at least some idea of the importance of recognizing the significance of death in particular and loss and grief more broadly. Bauman (2001) makes the point that:

> The thought of death and the experience of dying can kindle or strengthen the pleasure of being alive. ... And yet the dominant response of modernity is to forget and suppress, to bury death, to lock it up in the deepest vaults, the darkest memorial chambers of the self. May it rest there, until it rises again and the life of one's own ends. (p. 154)

Similarly, Saul Bellow described death as 'the dark backing a mirror needs if we are to see anything' (cited in Back, 2007, p. 4). The lesson I believe we can learn here – and it is one that the whole book reinforces – is that death in particular and the reality of loss as a feature of life in general are often difficult to face up to. But if we do not find the courage to do precisely that, to face up to the realities of our existence, then we will pay a high price – not least in being ill-equipped to deal with the challenges that loss and grief bring. Tillich, in what has come to be recognized as a classic work, argued that 'the courage to be' is in effect rooted in the courage to face up to nonbeing, to accept that we are finite beings who have to encounter death sooner or later (2000, originally published in 1952). In this way, Tillich reflects the general existentialist theme that we are enriched by making sure that we do not try to evade, through bad faith, the realities of what it means to be human (see Tomer, Eliason and Wong, 2008, for a range of discussions that reflect this theme). Holloway (2005) echoes a similar theme when he makes the very significant comment that: 'Our brief finitude is but a beautiful spark in the vast darkness of space. So we should live the fleeting day with passion and, when the night comes, depart from it with grace' (pp. 214–15).

In this book I have tried to present the harsh realities of a life that contains so many losses and thus so much grief, but I have tried to do so in a spirit of realism – that is, one that is not naively optimistic and prone to push into the background the grief-related aspects of human existence, nor unduly pessimistic and therefore dismissive of (or oblivious to) the joys and treasures (and thus richness of meaning) of being finite beings. Realism involves recognizing that the glass is both half full and half empty (Thompson, 2009b), that life is characterized by both pain and joy and that it is not helpful to see one while ignoring the other.

We have seen that grief is not a 'problem' as such (although it can cause immense difficulties), but rather a process of healing – healing the hurt that comes from having painful and distressing feelings imposed on us by one or more major losses. The tasks for professional helpers are mainly the following:

- To determine the difference between someone who is grieving without the need for professional help and who may therefore regard such help as intrusive and unnecessary and someone who is likely to come to harm (or cause harm to others) if the appropriate help is not forthcoming. Often the distinction is crystal clear and therefore relatively easy to make, but at times it can be a fine line to judge.
- Where it is clear that professional help is needed, to use our knowledge, skills and values sensitively in trying to help in

whatever reasonable ways we can to facilitate the healing process taking its course. In offering such help we need to recognize that different people grieve in different ways, and so we should not therefore try to force people to adopt what we see as the 'correct' way of grieving – it is more a case of helping them to find a pathway that works for them and, where necessary, to accompany them on at least part of that journey.

- To support colleagues in their efforts to meet the very demanding challenges of helping people cope with grief. It can be very helpful for all concerned if we can adopt an attitude of 'we are all in this together' and be ready to support one another, rather than make the mistake of assuming that needing help or support is a sign of weakness or professional inadequacy – it is simply a sign of being human.

- To make sure that we too are supported. Self-care, as we have noted, is a key element of effective practice. We cannot look after other people if we are not looking after ourselves. We take a big risk (which can backfire disastrously for the people we serve, for our employing organizations and, of course, for ourselves) if we try to deal with highly demanding forms of work without making sure that (i) we have the necessary support; and (ii) we are taking the necessary steps to ensure that our own needs – including emotional and spiritual needs – are being met.

We have also seen that, while grief is not in itself a problem, where there are complicating factors at work, the result can be serious personal and social problems that have the potential to devastate people's lives. So, while we should not lose sight of the fact that grieving is a healing process, we should also bear in mind that, where that healing is not happening for some reason, the consequences for the grieving person(s), for others and for society at large, can be hugely detrimental and can lead to further problems, sometimes setting off a very destructive vicious circle. Our task here, then, is to get the balance right, to allow the healing process of grief to flow freely without our interference where that is appropriate, and to intervene where we need to in those circumstances where healing is not happening – making sure that our interventions are based on:

- An adequate knowledge base and one that we keep adding to over time through continuous professional development and critically reflective practice;
- An adequate skills base that we will also build up over time, rather than complacently settle for what we already have;
- A commitment to our professional value base and the integrity to make sure that our actions are genuinely consistent with those values – recognizing that professional values are an important part of protecting vulnerable people from being exploited;
- A sensitivity to the need to support people gently and constructively, at a pace and in ways that they feel comfortable with; and
- The humility to recognize the limitations of what we can do, so that we do not give the people we serve false hopes and we do not set ourselves up to fail.

All this is a tall order, but in a sense that characterizes the book as a whole. Responding to the challenges of grief – whether directly in the form of coping with our own losses and the grief they bring or indirectly in the form of taking on the role of being a professional helper supporting others in their challenges – is certainly a tall order, a major undertaking. But, of course, it is also a vitally important part of being a helpful and compassionate human being, as well as being a highly rewarding enterprise that can bring immense personal and professional satisfaction, pride and a sense of doing something very, very worthwhile.

Guide to further learning

Further reading

The field of grief studies is blessed with a huge literature base, and so it needs to be understood that the selection of texts that follows is by no means comprehensive. It reflects to a large extent my own perspective, preferences and priorities. It should certainly not be assumed that anything that does not appear here is not worth reading. The reality is that there is so much important literature available to us that it is inevitable that some excellent reading materials will not be mentioned here.

Books

Children and young people

Corr, C. and Balk, D. (eds) (2010) *Children's Encounters with Death, Bereavement, and Coping*, New York, Springer.

Ribbens McCarthy, J. (2006) *Young People's Experience of Loss and Bereavement: Towards an Interdisciplinary Approach*, Maidenhead, Open University Press/McGraw-Hill Education.

Rowling, L. (2003) *Grief in School Communities: Effective Support Strategies*, Buckingham, Open University Press.

Tomlinson, P. and Philpot, T. (2008) *A Child's Journey to Recovery: Assessment and Planning with Traumatized Children*, London, Jessica Kingsley.

Coping and support

Berger, J. S. (2006) *Music of the Soul: Composing Life Out of Loss*, Abingdon, Routledge.

Corr, C. A., Nabe, C. M. and Corr, D. M. (2008) *Death and Dying, Life and Living*, 6th edn, Belmont, CA, Thomson Higher Education.

Currer, C. (2001) *Responding to Grief: Dying, Bereavement and Social Care*, Basingstoke, Palgrave Macmillan.

Gilbert, R. (1999) *Finding Your Way after Your Parent Dies: Help for Grieving Adults*, Notre Dame, IN, Ave Maria.

Hooyman, N. R. and Kramer, B. J. (2006) *Living Through Loss: Interventions Across the Lifespan*, New York, Columbia University Press.

Neimeyer, R. A. (2000) *Lessons of Loss: A Guide to Coping*, Memphis, TN, Center for the Study of Loss and Transition.

Smith, H. I. (2004) *Grievers Ask: Answers to Questions about Death and Loss*, Minneapolis, Augsburg Books.

Walter, C. A. and McCoyd, J. L. M. (2009) *Grief and Loss Across the Lifespan: A Biopsychosocial Perspective*, New York, Springer Publishing.

Weinstein, J. (2008) *Working with Loss, Death and Bereavement: A Guide for Social Workers*, London, Sage.

Crisis and trauma

Bracken, P. (2002) *Trauma: Culture, Meaning and Philosophy*, London, Whurr Publishers.

Everstine, D. S. and Everstine, L. (2006) *Strategic Interventions for People in Crisis, Trauma and Disaster*, Abingdon, Routledge.

Thompson, N. (2011) *Crisis Intervention*, 2nd edn, Lyme Regis, Russell House Publishing.

Warren, M. P. (2006) *From Trauma to Transformation*, Carmarthen, Crown House.

Wilson, J. P. (ed) (2006) *The Posttraumatic Self: Restoring Meaning and Wholeness to Personality*, London, Routledge.

Cultural diversity and grief

Chan, C. L. W. and Chow, A. Y. M. (eds) (2006) *Death, Dying and Bereavement: A Hong Kong Chinese Experience*, Hong Kong, Hong Kong University Press.

Morgan, J. and Laungani, P. (eds) (2002) *Death and Bereavement around the World: Vol 1, Major Religious Traditions*, Amityville, NY, Baywood.

Morgan, J. and Laungani, P. (eds.) (2003) *Death and Bereavement around the World: Vol 2, Death and Bereavement in the Americas,* Amityville, NY, Baywood.

Morgan, J. and Laungani, P. (eds) (2004) *Death and Bereavement around the World: Vol 3, Death and Bereavement in Europe*, Amityville, NY, Baywood.

Morgan, J. and Laungani, P. (eds) (2004) *Death and Bereavement around the World: Vol 4, Death and Bereavement in Asia, Australia and New Zealand*, Amityville, NY, Baywood.

Morgan, J., Laungani, P. and Palmer, S. (eds) (2009) *Death and Bereavement Around the World: Volume 5, Reflective Essays*, Amityville, NY, Baywood.

Parkes, C. M., Laungani, P. and Young, B. (eds.) (1997) *Death and Bereavement Across Cultures*, London, Routledge.

Existential and spiritual issues

Cobb, M. (2001) *The Dying Soul: Spiritual Care at the End of Life*, Buckingham, Open University Press.

Cox, G., Bendiksen, R. and Stevenson, R. (eds) (2003) *Making Sense of Death: Spiritual, Pastoral, and Personal Aspects of Death, Dying and Bereavement*, Amityville, NY, Baywood.

Doka, K. and Morgan, J. (eds) (1993) *Death and Spirituality,* Amityville, NY, Baywood.

Thompson, N. (2007) 'Loss and Grief: Spiritual Aspects', in Coyte, M. E., Gilbert, P. and Nicholls, V. (eds) (2007) *Spirituality, Values and Mental Health*, London, Jessica Kingsley.

Thompson, N. and Walsh, M. (2010) 'The Existential Basis of Trauma', *Journal of Social Work Practice*, 24(4).

Tomer, A., Eliason, G. T. and Wong, P. T. P. (eds) (2008) *Existential and Spiritual Issues in Death Attitudes*, New York, Lawrence Erlbaum Associates.

Grief in the workplace

Davidson, J. D. and Doka, K. (eds) (1999) *Living with Grief: At Work, at School, at Worship*, Levittown, PA, Brunner/Mazel.

Tehrani, N. (2004) *Workplace Trauma: Concepts, Assessment and Interventions*, New York, Brunner-Routledge.

Thompson, N. (2009) *Loss, Grief and Trauma in the Workplace*, Amityville, NY, Baywood.

Loss and grief generally

Berzoff, J. and Silverman, P. (eds) (2004) *Living with Dying: A Comprehensive Resource for Health Care Professionals*, New York, Columbia University Press.

Bryant, C. and Peck, D. (eds) (2009) *Encyclopedia of Death and the Human Experience,* Thousand Oaks, CA, Sage.

DeSpelder, L. A. and Strickland, A. L. (2005) *The Last Dance: Encountering Death and Dying*, 7th edn, London, McGraw-Hill Higher Education.

Dickenson, D., Johnson, M. and Katz, J. S. (eds) (2000) *Death, Dying and Bereavement*, London, Sage.

Howarth, G. and Leaman, O. (eds) (2001) *Encyclopedia of Death and Dying*, New York, Routledge.

Klass, D., Silverman, P. and Nickman, S. (eds) (1996) *Continuing Bonds: New Understandings of Grief*, Washington, DC, Taylor & Francis.

Neimeyer, R. A. (2001) *Meaning Reconstruction and the Experience of Loss*, Washington, DC, American Psychological Association.

Neimeyer, R. A., Harris, D. L., Winokuer, H. R. and Thornton, G. F. (2011) *Grief and Bereavement in Contemporary Society*, New York, Routledge.

Spiro, H. M., McCrea Curnen, M. G. and Wandel, L. P. (eds) (1996) *Facing Death*, New Haven, CT, Yale University Press.

Thompson, N. (ed.) (2002) *Loss and Grief: A Guide for Human Services Practitioners*, Basingstoke, Palgrave Macmillan.

Self-care

Papatadou, D. (2009) *In the Face of Death: Professionals who Care for the Dying and the Bereaved*, New York, NY, Springer Publishing.

Renzenbrink, I. (ed.) (2011) *Caregiver Stress and Staff Support in Illness, Dying and Bereavement*, Oxford, Oxford University Press.

The social context of grief

Doka, K. J. and Martin, T. L. (2010) *Grieving Beyond Gender: Understanding the Ways Men and Women Mourn*, 2nd edn, New York, Routledge.

Howarth, G. (2007) *Death and Dying: A Sociological Introduction*, Cambridge, Polity Press.

Howarth, G. and Jupp, P. C. (1996) *Contemporary Issues in the Sociology of Death, Dying and Disposal*, Basingstoke, Macmillan.

Kellehear, A. (2005) *Compassionate Cities: Public Health and End-of-life Care*, Abingdon, Routledge.

Kellehear, A. (2007) *A Social History of Dying*, Cambridge, Cambridge University Press.

Rosenblatt, P. C. and Wallace, B. R. (2005) *African American Grief*, Hove, Routledge.

Stories of loss

Attig. T. (2002) *The Heart of Grief: Death and the Search for Lasting Love*, Oxford, Oxford University Press.

Attig, T. (2011) *How We Grieve: Relearning the World*, 2nd edn, Oxford, Oxford University Press.

Bird, C. (ed.) (1998) *The Stolen Children: Their Stories*, Milsons Point, NSW, Random House.

Canfield, J. and Hansen, M. V. (2003) *Chicken Soup for the Grieving Soul: Stories About Life, Death and Overcoming the Loss of a Loved One*, Dearfield Beach, FL, Health Communications.

Carol, J. (2004) *Journeys of Courage: Remarkable Stories of the Healing Power of Community*, Notre Dame, IN, Sorin Books.

Gelfand, D. E., Raspa, R., Briller, S. H. and Myers Schin, S. (eds) (2005) *End-of-Life Stories: Crossing Disciplinary Boundaries*, New York, NY, Springer Publishing.

Hedtke, L. and Winslade, J. (2004) *Re-Membering Lives: Conversation with the Dying and the Bereaved*, Amityvillle, NY, Baywood Publishing.

Suicide

Lukas, C. and Seiden, H. M. (2007) *Silent Grief: Living in the Wake of Suicide*, London, Jessica Kingsley Publishers.
Wertheimer, A. (2001) *A Special Scar: The Experiences of People Bereaved by Suicide*, 2nd edn, Hove, Brunner-Routledge.

Transformational grief

Calhoun, L. and Tedeschi, R. (1999) *Facilitating Posttraumatic Growth: A Clinician's Guide*, Mahwah, NJ, Lawrence Erlbaum Associates.
Calhoun, L. and Tedeschi, R. (2001) 'Posttraumatic Growth: The Positive Lessons of Loss', in Neimeyer, R. A. (ed.) (2001) *Meaning Reconstruction and the Experience of Loss*, Washington, DC, American Psychological Association.
Schneider, J. M. (2000) *The Overdiagnosis of Depression: Recognizing Grief and Its Transformative Potential*, Traverse City, MI, Seasons Press.
Schneider, J. (2006) *Transforming Loss: A Discovery Process,* East Lansing, MI, Integra Press.

Journals

Crisis – The Journal of Crisis Intervention and Suicide Prevention, http://www.hhpub.com/journals/crisis/
Crisis Intervention and Time-Limited Treatment, http://www.ingentaconnect.com/content/tandf/gcit
Death Studies, http://www.tandf.co.uk/journals/titles/07481187.asp
Grief Matters: The Australian Journal of Grief and Bereavement, http://www.grief.org.au/grief_matters.html
Illness, Crisis & Loss, http://baywood.com/journals/

Journal of Loss and Trauma: International Perspectives on Stress and Coping, www.tandf.co.uk/journals/titles/15325024.asp

Mortality, www.tandf.co.uk/journals/titles/13576275.asp

OMEGA – Journal of Death and Dying, http://baywood.com/journals/PreviewJournals.asp?Id=0030-2228

Training and development resources

Moss, B. (2010) *Responding to Loss: A Learning and Development Manual*, Lyme Regis, Russell House Publishing.

Thompson, N. (2010) *Working with Grief*, a DVD produced by Avenue Media Solutions (www.avenuemediasolutions.com).

Websites

The website, www.griefchallenges.com <http://www.griefchallenges.com> is a companion resource to this book. Other useful websites include:

The American Academy of Experts in Traumatic Stress, www.aaets.org

American Psychological Association Disaster Response Network, www.apa.org

Association for Death Education and Counseling (ADEC), www.adec.org

Australian Centre for Grief and Bereavement, www.grief.org.au

The Compassionate Friends, www.compassionatefriends.org

The Dougy Center for Grieving Children and Families, www.dougy.org

Genesis Bereavement Resources, www.genesis-resources.com

Gift from Within, www.giftfromwithin.org

International Critical Incident Stress Foundation, www.icisf.org

The International Work Group on Death, Dying and Bereavement, www.iwgddb.org

Living with Loss Foundation, www.livingwithloss.org

National Center for Post-Traumatic Stress Disorders, www.ncptsd.org

The Solace Tree (for grieving children and adolescents), www.solacetree.org

Tragedy Assistance Program for Survivors, www.taps.org

The Workplace Trauma Center, www.workplacetraumacenter.com

References

Amiel, S. and Heath, I. (eds) (2003) *Family Violence in Primary Care*, Oxford, Oxford University Press.

Atkinson, J. (2002) *Trauma Trails: Recreating Song Lines The Transgenerational Effects of Trauma in Indigenous Australia*, Melbourne, Spinifex.

Attig, T. (2001) 'Relearning the World: Making and Finding Meanings', in Neimeyer (2001).

Attig. T. (2002) *The Heart of Grief: Death and the Search for Lasting Love*, Oxford, Oxford University Press.

Attig, T. (2011), *How We Grieve: Relearning the World*, 2nd edn, Oxford and New York, Oxford University Press.

Auger, J. A. (2000) *Social Perspectives on Death and Dying*, Halifax, Canada, Fernwood Publishing.

Back, L. (2007) *The Art of Listening*, New York, Berg.

Back, L. and Solomos, J. (eds) (2009) *Theories of Race and Racism: A Reader*, 2nd edn, London, Routledge.

Barbalet, J. (ed.) (2002) *Emotions and Sociology*, Oxford, Blackwell.

Barrett, R. K. (1998) 'Sociocultural Considerations for Working with Blacks Experiencing Loss and Grief', in Doka and Davidson (1998).

Baum, N. (2003) 'The Male Way of Divorce: When, What and How', *Clinical Social Work Journal*, 31(1).

Bauman, Z. (1991) *Modernity and the Holocaust*, Cambridge, Polity.

Baumeister, R. F. (2001) *Evil: Inside Human Violence and Cruelty*, New York, Henry Holt.

Berzoff, J. and Silverman, P. R. (eds) (2004) *Living with Dying: A Handbook for End-of-Life Healthcare Practitioners*, New York, Columbia University Press.

Bevan, D. (2002) 'Poverty and Deprivation', in Thompson (2002).

Bocknek, E., Sanderson, J. and Britner, P. (2009) 'Ambiguous Loss and Posttraumatic Stress in School-Age Children of Prisoners', *Journal of Child & Family Studies*, 18(3).

Bonanno, G. A. (2009) *The Other Side of Sadness: What the New Science of Bereavement Tells Us About Life After Loss*, New York, Basic Books.

Bowlby, J. (1981) *Loss: Sadness and Depression*, Harmondsworth, Penguin.

Bracher, M. (2009) *Social Symptoms of Identity Needs: Why We Have Failed to Solve Our Social Problems and What to Do About It*, London, Karnac.

Bracken, P. (2003) *Trauma: Culture, Meaning and Philosophy*, London, Whurr.

Brandon, D. (2000) *Tao of Survival: Spirituality in Social Care and Counselling*, Birmingham, Venture Press.

Buber, M. (2004) *I and Thou*, London, Continuum.

187

Calhoun, L. G. and Tedeschi, R. G. (2001) 'Posttraumatic Growth: The Positive Lessons of Loss', in Neimeyer (2001b).

Carabine, J. (ed.) (2004) *Sexualities: Personal Lives and Social Policy*, Bristol, The Policy Press.

Castiglione, D., van Deth, J. W. and Wolleb, G. (eds) (2008) *The Handbook of Social Capital*, Oxford, Oxford University Press.

Chan, C. L. W. and Chow, A. Y. M. (eds) (2006) *Death, Dying and Bereavement: A Hong Kong Chinese Experience*, Hong Kong, Hong Kong University Press.

Clarke, J. (2001) 'Social Problems: Sociological Perspectives', in May, Page and Brunsdon (2001).

Cohen, C. I. and Timini, S. (eds) (2008) *Liberatory Psychiatry: Philosophy, Politics and Mental Health*, Cambridge, Cambridge University Press.

Corby, B. (2005) *Child Abuse: Towards a Knowledge Base*, 3rd edn, Maidenhead, Open University Press.

Corr, C. (1998) 'Enhancing the Concept of Disenfranchised Grief', paper presented at the annual meeting of the Association for Death Education and Counseling, Chicago, IL, March.

Corr, C., Nabe, C. M. and Corr, D. (2008) *Death and Dying, Life and Living*, 6th edn, Belmont, CA, Thomson Wadsworth.

Cox, G., Bendiksen, R. and Stevenson, R. (eds) (2002) *Complicated Grieving and Bereavement: Understanding and Treating People Experiencing Loss*, Amityville, NY, Baywood.

Craib, I. (1998) *Experiencing Identity*, London, Sage.

Cranwell-Ward, J. and Abbey, A. (2005) *Organizational Stress*, Basingstoke, Palgrave Macmillan.

Coyte, M. E., Gilbert, P. and Nicholls, V. (eds) (2007) *Spirituality, Values and Mental Health*, London, Jessica Kingsley.

Currer, C. (2001) *Responding to Grief: Dying, Bereavement and Social Care*, Basingstoke, Palgrave Macmillan.

Davidson, J. D. and Doka, K. (eds) (1999) *Living with Grief: At Work, at School, at Worship*, Levittown, PA, Brunner/Mazel.

Dawes, J. (2002) 'Losses and Justice: An Australian Perspective', in Thompson (2002).

Denney, D. (2005) *Risk and Society*, London, Sage.

Desai, S. and Bevan, D. (2002) 'Race and Culture', in Thompson (2002).

DeSpelder, L. A. and Strickland, A. L. (2005) *The Last Dance: Encountering Death and Dying*, 7th edn, New York, McGraw-Hill.

Dickenson, D., Johnson, M and Katz, J. S. (eds) (2000) *Death, Dying and Bereavement*, London, Sage.

Doka, K. (ed.) (1989) *Disenfranchised Grief: Recognizing Hidden Sorrow*, San Francisco, CA, Jossey Bass.

Doka, K. J. (1999) 'A Primer on Loss and Grief', in Davidson and Doka (1999).

Doka, K. J. (ed.) (2000) *Living with Grief: Children, Adolescents and Loss*, Washington, DC, Hospice Foundation of America.

Doka, K. J. (2002) *Disenfranchised Grief: New Directions, Challenges, and Strategies for Practice*, Champaign, IL, Research Press.

Doka, K. J. and Davidson, J. D. (eds) (1998) *Living with Grief: Who We Are, How We Grieve*, Philadelphia, PA, Brunner/Mazel.

Doka, K. J. and Jendreski, M. (1988) 'Clergy Understanding of Grief, Bereavement and Mourning', *Research Record*, 2(4), pp. 105–12.

Doka, K. J. and Martin, T. L. (2010) *Grieving Beyond Gender: Understanding the Ways Men and Women Mourn*, 2nd edn, New York, Routledge.

Eliason, G. T., Lepore, M. and Myer, R. (2008) 'The Historical Advancement of Grief Counseling', in Tomer, Eliason and Wong (2008).

Everstine, D. S. and Everstine, L. (2006) *Strategic Interventions for People in Crisis, Trauma and Disaster*, Abingdon, Routledge.

Figley, C. R. (1999) 'Compassion Fatigue: Toward a New Understanding of the Costs of Caring', in Stamm (1999).

Fineman, S. (ed.) (2000) *Emotion in Organizations*, 2nd edn, London, Sage.

Fischer, A. (ed.) (2000) *Gender and Emotion: Social Psychological Perspectives*, Cambridge, Cambridge University Press.

Fleming, S. J. and Belanger, S. K. (2001) 'Trauma, Grief, and Surviving Child Sexual Abuse', in Neimeyer (2001).

Furedi, F. (2004) *Therapy Culture: Cultivating Vulnerability in an Uncertain Age*, London, Routledge.

Goldman, L. (2002) *Breaking the Silence: A Guide to Helping Children with Complicated Grief – Suicide, Homicide, AIDS, Violence and Abuse*, New York, Routledge.

Goleman, D. (1996) *Emotional Intelligence: Why it Can Matter More than IQ*, London, Bloomsbury.

Guirdham, M. (1999) *Communicating Across Cultures*, Basingstoke, Macmillan – now Palgrave Macmillan.

Hamer, M. (2006) *The Barefoot Helper*, Lyme Regis, Russell House Publishing.

Hames, C. C. and Pedreira, D. (2003) 'Children with Parents in Prison: Disenfranchised Grievers who Benefit from Bibliotherapy', *Illness, Crisis & Loss*, 11(4).

Harvey, J. H. (2002) *Perspectives on Loss and Trauma: Assaults on the Self*, London, Sage.

Hedtke, L. and Winslade, J. (2004) *Re-Membering Lives: Conversations with the Dying and the Bereaved*, Amityville, NY, Baywood.

Hockey, J. (1996) 'The View from the West: Reading the Anthropology on Non-Western Death Ritual', in Howarth and Jupp (1996).

Holloway, M. and Moss, B. (2010) *Spirituality and Social Work*, Basingstoke, Palgrave Macmillan.

Holloway, R. (2005) *Looking in the Distance: The Human Search for Meaning*, Edinburgh, Canongate.

Hooyman, N. R. and Kramer, B. J. (2006) *Living Through Loss: Interventions Across the Lifespan*, New York, Columbia University Press.

Howarth, G. (2007) *Death and Dying: A Sociological Introduction*, Cambridge, Polity Press.

Howarth, G. and Jupp, P. C. (eds) (1996) *Contemporary Issues in the Sociology of Death, Dying and Disposal*, Basingstoke, Macmillan.

Kellehear, A. (2005) *Compassionate Cities: Public Health and End-of-life Care*, London, Routledge.

Kellehear, A. (2007) *A Social History of Dying*, Cambridge, Cambridge University Press.

Klass, D., Silverman, P. R. and Nickman, S. (eds) (1996) *Continuing Bonds: New Understandings of Grief*, Washington, DC, Taylor & Francis.

Kroll, B. (2002) 'Children and Divorce', in Thompson (2002c).

Kübler-Ross, E. (1969) *On Death and Dying*, New York, Macmillan.

Lattanzi-Licht, M. and Doka, K. J. (eds) (2003) *Coping with Public Tragedy*, New York, Brunner-Routledge.

Lawler, S. (2008) *Identity: Sociological Perspectives*, Cambridge, Polity.

Leach, R. M., Burgess, T. and Holmwood, C. (2008) 'Could Recidivism in Prisoners Be Linked to Traumatic Grief? A Review of the Evidence', *International Journal of Prisoner Health*, 4(2).

Lin, N. (2001) *Social Capital: A Theory of Social Structure and Action*, Cambridge, Cambridge University Press.

Lister, R. (2004) *Poverty*, Cambridge, Polity.

Machin, L. (2008) *Working with Loss and Grief*, London, Sage.

Malik, K. (1996) *The Meaning of Race: Race, History and Culture in Western Society*, Basingstoke, Macmillan.

Malik, K. (2008) *Strange Fruit: Why Both Sides are Wrong in the Race Debate*, Oxford, Oneworld.

Marris, P. (1974) *Loss and Change*, 2nd edn, London Routledge & Kegan Paul.

Martin, J. (2007) *Safeguarding Adults*, Lyme Regis, Russell House Publishing.

Maslach, C. (1982) *Burnout: The Cost of Caring*, Englewood Cliffs, NJ, Prentice Hall.

May, M., Page, R. and Brunsdon, E. (eds) (2001) *Understanding Social Problems: Issues in Social Policy*, Oxford, Blackwell.

McBride, J. and Johnson, E. D. (2005) 'Crisis Intervention, Grief Therapy, and the Loss of Life', in Roberts (2005).

Miller, D. (2000) *Dying to Care? Work, Stress and Burnout in HIV/AIDS*, London, Routledge.

Moss, B. (2002) 'Spirituality: A Personal Perspective', in Thompson (2002).

Moss, B. (2005) *Spirituality and Religion*, Lyme Regis, Russell House Publishing.

Moss, B. (2007a) 'Guest Editorial', *Illness, Crisis & Loss*, 15(2).

Moss, B. (2007b) 'Illness, Crisis and Loss: Towards a Spiritually Intelligent Workplace', *Illness, Crisis & Loss*, 15(3).

Neimeyer, R. A. (2000) *Lessons of Loss: A Guide to Coping*, Memphis, TN, Center for the Study of Loss and Transition.

Neimeyer, R. A. (2001a) 'Introduction: Meaning Reconstruction and Loss', in Neimeyer (2001b).

Neimeyer, R. A. (ed.) (2001b) *Meaning Reconstruction and the Experience of Loss*, Washington, DC, American Psychological Association.

Neimeyer, R. A. (2006) 'Foreword', in Chan and Chow (2006).

Neimeyer, R. A. and Anderson, A. (2002) 'Meaning Reconstruction Theory', in Thompson (2002).

Neimeyer, R. A., Harris, D. L., Winokuer, H. R. and Thornton, G. F. (2011) *Grief and Bereavement in Contemporary Society*, New York, Routledge.

Nicholls, V. (2007) 'Loss and its Truths: Spirituality, Loss and Mental Health', *Illness, Crisis & Loss* 15(2).

Nouwen, H. (1996) *The Wounded Healer: Ministry in Contemporary Society*, London, Darton, Longman & Todd.

Oatley, K., Keltner, D. and Jenkins, J. M. (2006) *Understanding Emotions*, London, John Wiley & Son.

O'Halloran, M. S., Ingala, A. M., and Copeland, E. P. (2005) 'Crisis Intervention with Early Adolescents who Have Suffered a Significant Loss', in Roberts (2005).

Oliver, M. (2004) 'If I Had a Hammer: The Social Model in Action', in Swain et al. (2004).

Oliver, M. and Sapey, B. (2006) *Social Work with Disabled People*, 3rd edn, Basingstoke, Palgrave Macmillan.

Palmer, P. (1998) *The Courage to Teach: Exploring the Inner Landscape of a Teacher's Life*, San Francisco, CA, Jossey-Bass.

Papadatou, D. (2009) *In the Face of Death: Professionals who Care for the Dying and Bereaved*, New York, Springer.

Parekh, B. (2008) *A New Politics of Identity: Political Principles for an Interdependent World*, Basingstoke, Palgrave Macmillan.

Parkes, C. M. (2008) 'Making and Breaking Cycles of Violence', in Stevenson and Cox (2008).

Payne, G. (2006) *Social Divisions*, Basingstoke, Palgrave Macmillan.

Pullen, A., Beech, N. and Sims, D. (2007) *Exploring Identity: Concepts and Methods*, Basingstoke, Palgrave Macmillan.

Radford, L. (2001) 'Domestic Violence', in May, Page and Brunsdon (2001).

Rando, T. A. (1993) *Treatment of Complicated Mourning*, Champaign, IL, Research Press.

Rando, T. A. (2000a) 'On the Experience of Traumatic Stress in Anticipatory and Postdeath Mourning', in Rando (2000b).

Rando, T. A. (ed.) (2000b) *Clinical Dimensions of Anticipatory Mourning: Theory and Practice in Working with the Dying, their Loved Ones, and their Caregivers*, Champaign, IL, Research Press.

Rando, T. A. (2003) 'Public Tragedy and Complicated Mourning', in Lattanzi-Licht and Doka (2003).

Renzenbrink, I. (2004) 'Relentless Self-care', in Berzoff and Silverman (2004).

Renzenbrink, I. (ed.) (2011) *Caregiver Stress and Staff Support in Illness, Dying and Bereavement,* Oxford, Oxford University Press.

Riches, G. (2002) 'Gender and Sexism', in Thompson (2002).

Riches, G. and Dawson, P. (2000) *An Intimate Loneliness*, Buckingham, Open University Press.

Roberts, A. R. (ed.) (2005) *Crisis Intervention Handbook: Assessment, Treatment, and Research*, 3rd edn, New York, Oxford University Press.

Rosenblatt, P. and Wallace, B. R. (2005) *African American Grief*, London and New York, Routledge.

Rowling, L. (2003) *Grief in School Communities: Effective Support Strategies*, Buckingham, Open University Press.

Rymaszewska, J. and Philpot, T. (2006) *Reaching the Vulnerable Child: Therapy with Traumatized Children*, London, Jessica Kingsley.

Sapey, B. (2002) 'Disability', in Thompson (2002).

Sartorius, N. (2003) 'Social Capital and Mental Health', *Current Opinion in Psychiatry*, 16, Supplement 2.

Schneider, J. (2000) *The Overdiagnosis of Depression: Recognizing Grief and its Transformative Potential*, Traverse City, MI, Seasons Press.

Schneider, J. (2006) *Transforming Loss: A Discovery Process*, East Lansing, MI, Integra Press.

Sibeon, R. (2004) *Rethinking Social Theory*, London, Sage.

Smith, H. K and Smith, M. K. (2008) *The Art of Helping Others: Being Around, Being There, Being Wise*, London, Jessica Kingsley.

Stamm, B. H. (ed.) (1999) *Secondary Traumatic Stress: Self-Care Issues for Clinicians, Researchers, and Educators*, 2nd edn, Baltimore, MD, Sidran Press.

Stevenson, R. G. (2000) 'The Role of Death Education in Helping Students to Cope with Loss', in Doka (2000).

Stevenson, R. G. and Cox, G. R. (eds) (2008) *Perspectives on Violence and Violent Death*, Amityville, NY, Baywood.

Stroebe, M. and Schut, H. (1999) 'The Dual Process Model of Coping with Bereavement: Rationale and Description', *Death Studies*, 23(3).

Sutherland, V. J. and Cooper, C. L. (2000) *Strategic Stress Management: An Organizational Approach*, Basingstoke: Macmillan – now Palgrave Macmillan.

Swain, J, French, S., Barnes, C. and Thomas, C. (eds) (2004) *Disabling Barriers – Enabling Environments*, 2nd edn, London, Sage.

Swift, K. J. and Callahan, M. (2009) *At Risk: Social Justice in Child Welfare and Other Human Services*, Toronto, University of Toronto Press.

Tehan, M. (2007) 'The Compassionate Workplace: Leading with the Heart', *Illness, Crisis & Loss*, 15(3).

Terrell, F. and Barrett, R. K. (1979) 'Interpersonal Trust among College Students as a Function of Race, Sex and Socioeconomic Class', *Perceptual and Motor Skills*, 48.

Terrell, F. and Terrell, S. (1983) 'The Relationship between Race of Examiner,

Cultural Mistrust, and the Intelligence Test Results of Black Children', *Psychology in the Schools*, 20: 367–9.

Thomas, P. and Bracken, P. (2008) 'Power, Freedom, and Mental Health', in Cohen and Timini (2008).

Thompson, B. and Colón, Y. (2004) 'Lesbians and Gay Men at the End of Their Lives: Psychosocial Concerns', in Berzoff and Silverman (2004).

Thompson, H. S. (2003) *Hell's Angels*, London, Penguin.

Thompson, N. (1999) *Stress Matters*, Pepar Publications, available from http://www.avenueconsulting.co.uk/neil-thompson/books.html#offer

Thompson, N. (2000) *Theory and Practice in Human Services*, 2nd edn, Buckingham, Open University Press.

Thompson, N. (ed.) (2002) *Loss and Grief: A Guide for Human Services Practitioners*, Basingstoke, Palgrave Macmillan.

Thompson, N. (2007) *Power and Empowerment*, Lyme Regis, Russell House Publishing.

Thompson, N. (2007) 'Loss and Grief: Spiritual Aspects', in Coyte et al. (2007).

Thompson, N. (2009a) *Loss, Grief and Trauma in the Workplace*, Amityville, NY, Baywood.

Thompson, N. (2009b) *People Skills*, 3rd edn, Basingstoke, Palgrave Macmillan.

Thompson, N. (2009c) *Practising Social Work: Meeting the Professional Challenge*, Basingstoke, Palgrave Macmillan.

Thompson, N. (2009d) 'Stress', in Thompson and Bates (2009).

Thompson, N. (2010) *Theorizing Social Work Practice*, Basingstoke, Palgrave Macmillan.

Thompson, N. (2011a) *Crisis Intervention*, 2nd edn, Lyme Regis, Russell House Publishing.

Thompson, N. (2011b) *Promoting Equality: Working with Diversity and Difference*, 3rd edn, Basingstoke, Palgrave Macmillan.

Thompson, N. (2011c) *Effective Communication*, 2nd edn, Basingstoke, Palgrave Macmillan.

Thompson, N. (2012) *Anti-Discriminatory Practice*, 5th edn, Basingstoke, Palgrave Macmillan.

Thompson, N. and Bates, J. (eds) (2009) *Promoting Workplace Well-being*, Basingstoke, Palgrave Macmillan.

Thompson, N. and Thompson, S. (2008) *The Social Work Companion*, Basingstoke, Palgrave Macmillan.

Thompson, N. and Walsh, M. (2010) 'The Existential Basis of Trauma', *Journal of Social Work Practice* 24(4).

Thompson, S. (2007) 'Spirituality and Old Age', *Illness, Crisis & Loss*, 15(2).

Thompson, S. and Thompson, N. (2004) 'Working with Dying and Bereaved Older People', in Berzoff and Silverman (2004).

Thompson, S. and Thompson, N. (2008) *The Critically Reflective Practitioner*, Basingstoke, Palgrave Macmillan.

Tillich, P. (2000) *The Courage to Be*, 2nd edn, New Haven, NJ, Yale University Press.

Tomer, A., Eliason, G. T. and Wong, P. T. P. (eds) (2008) *Existential and Spiritual Issues in Death Attitudes*, New York, Lawrence Erlbaum Associates.

Tomlinson, P. and Philpot, T. (2008) *A Child's Journey to Recovery: Assessment and Planning with Traumatized Children*, London, Jessica Kingsley.

Ungunmerr-Baumann, Miriam-Rose (1988) *Ngangikurungkurr Deep Water Sounds*, Hobart, International Liturgy Assembly, NTC 232 UNGU.

Unamuno, M. de (1954) *Tragic Sense of Life*, New York, Dover Publications.

Walter, C. A. and McCoyd, J. L. M. (2009) *Grief and Loss across the Lifespan: A Biopsychosocial Perspective*, New York, Springer.

Walter, T. (1994) *The Revival of Death*, London, Routledge.

Warren, M. P. (2006) *From Trauma to Transformation*, Carmarthen, Crown House.

Weinstein, J. (2008) *Working with Loss, Death and Bereavement: A Guide for Social Workers*, London, Sage.

Wertheimer, A. (2001) *A Special Scar: The Experience of People Bereaved by Suicide*, 2nd edn, Hove, Brunner-Routledge.

Wicks, R. (2002) *Nietzsche*, Oxford, Oneworld.

Wilson, J. P. (ed) (2006) *The Posttraumatic Self: Restoring Meaning and Wholeness to Personality*, London, Routledge.

Worden, J. W. (2009 [1983]) *Grief Counselling and Grief Therapy: A Handbook for the Mental Health Practitioner*, 4th edn, London, Routledge.

Žižek, S. (2010) *Living in the End Times*, London, Verso.

Zohar, D. and Marshall, I. (2000) *SQ: Connecting with our Spiritual Intelligence*, London. Bloomsbury.

Zohar, D, and Marshall, I. (2004) *Spiritual Capital: Wealth we Can Live By*, London, Bloomsbury.

Index